GW00505669

DRIVE AROUND SWEDEN

A handy guide for the motorist

ROBERT SPARK

TRAFTON PUBLISHING

Companion volumes:

DRIVE AROUND DENMARK
DRIVE AROUND NORWAY

FOR MYRNA

First published 1986
Reprinted 1989

Photographs: pages 33,34 (upper) - Scandinavian Seaways;
pages 36, 69, 71 (lower), 73, 75 (upper), 76, 112 - Swedish
Tourist Board; page 71 (upper) - David Cockroft; pages 34
(lower), 72, 74, 75 (lower), 109, 110, 111 - author.

Cover: A typical well-surfaced road in northern Sweden with a
reindeer enjoying the roadside greenery. Photograph by the
author.

Design: Peter Kerr Design Associates Ltd., 89A Quicks Road,
London SW19 1EX.
Typeset by Ian Greig Ltd, 132 Anyards Road, Cobham, Surrey.
Printed in Great Britain by Butler & Tanner Ltd, Frome,
Somerset.

CONTENTS

AN INTRODUCTION TO SWEDEN

IT IS NO exaggeration to call Sweden Europe's unknown holiday destination. The number of British visitors is relatively small and those driving around Sweden even smaller. Yet there is no reason why this should be so. It is accessible, with frequent sailings by large well-equipped car ferries and it offers no great driving problems.

There are thousands of miles of well-surfaced roads with comparatively little traffic, while the range of accommodation is wide and the standard universally high. Food is enjoyable and very much to our taste. There is an abundance of things to see and do and English is widely spoken. The long-held image of Sweden as an expensive country is no longer valid; it now offers good value for money.

The Swedish people have had something of a reputation for being reserved, but this, too, has changed and the visitor, certainly from these shores, will receive a friendly welcome.

A BIG COUNTRY

Sweden is the largest of the Scandinavian countries and the fourth largest European country (after Russia, France and Spain). From north to south it is almost 1,000 miles in length and has an area of 173,654 square miles (449,793 square kilometres).

There are some 96,000 lakes, about 150,000 islands (even if some of them are very small) while the coastline extends for a distance of 4,200 miles.

Broadly speaking Sweden is less hilly in the south, more mountainous along its western border with Norway and in the north. But this does not mean that the southern half of the country is dull, because much of the countryside is nicely undulating. The mountains are, in the main, fairly gentle, the most impressive being in the far north which is where you will find the highest peak, *Kebnekaise* (6,942 ft above sea level).

Although Sweden is almost twice the area of the British Isles, the population of 8.3 million is no larger than that of Greater London. When you also take into account that over 25 per cent of the population lives in the three largest cities (Stockholm, Gothenburg and Malmö), it is easy to understand why one of the joys of Sweden is that there is plenty of breathing space.

The scenery is varied: immense forests (they cover 50 per cent of the country), tranquil lakes, rich farmland, fast flowing rivers and surging waterfalls and the vast emptiness of the northern uplands. The coastline ranges from inviting sandy beaches to cliffs and rocky coves, not to mention the fascinating archipelagos – especially the one close to Stockholm with its 22,000 islands.

The forests, lakes and wide open spaces contrast with the towns which reflect the high standard of living enjoyed by the Swedish people. Industry is also present of course, because Sweden is a technological nation, but factories are usually found on the outskirts of towns and cities. Only on rare occasions does industry impinge on the delights of the countryside and coastline. It certainly is not allowed to pollute the environment: air and water are pure. Sweden has affluence but not effluent.

SEEING SWEDEN

During the average length of holiday you will only be able to drive around part of Sweden. As you cannot cover it all, use this guide to decide which area of the country appeals to you.

Although distances are considerable, the excellent highways and the modest amount of traffic lets you cover the ground without undue difficulty. But the enjoyment of your motoring holiday is to explore, using the smaller roads and getting away from the mainstream of traffic.

Apart from a few popular places in peak summer, Sweden is never overwhelmed by holidaymakers (domestic or foreign). There is, in the rural areas, a great sense of tranquillity which allows you to relax and enjoy yourself.

PARTS OF SWEDEN

Sweden is divided into 24 counties or provinces called *Län* which are shown on the map on page 9. Of course the visitor need not take too much notice of these boundaries, although they make a convenient way of highlighting the various parts of the country.

The west coast of Sweden stretches for 250 miles and embraces the counties of *Bohuslän* and *Halland*. The former has a rocky coastline while the latter includes many beaches. The entire coast is a popular summer holiday area and roughly midway along it is Gothenburg, Sweden's second largest city and the principal port of entry for the British motorist.

Skåne, in the south-east, is Sweden's castle and manor house county and it retains a slightly Danish atmosphere, a hangover from when it was part of Denmark. There is a nice combination of rich farmland and undulating hills while the province includes Malmö, Sweden's third largest city, and Lund, one of the country's most historic towns.

Adjoining Skåne and the little county of Blekinge is *Småland*, which enjoys such a variety of scenery that it has been dubbed 'Sweden in miniature'. West of the fortress town of Kalmar is the 'Kingdom of Glass', the home of Sweden's glass-making industry. *Växjö* is an interesting centre, while at the southern tip of Lake Vättern is *Jönköping*, where the Swedish match industry was established. On the shores of Lake Vättern are two picturesque little towns: *Gränna* (facing the enchanting island of Visingsö) and (in Östergötland) *Vadstena* with its medieval atmosphere.

Off the east coast is the long thin island of *Öland*, which is claimed to be the warmest and sunniest part of Sweden and whose landscape is dotted with some 400 windmills. To the north-east of

Öland is *Gotland*, Sweden's largest island which has its own distinctive personality. The principal town, *Visby*, was once an important Hanseatic trading centre.

Between Lakes Vättern and Vänern in Västergötland there is some very explorable countryside, while *Hjo* and *Karlsborg* (on Vättern) and *Läckö* Castle and *Mariestad* (on Vänern) are definitely worth a visit. Further west is the beautiful county of *Värmland* with its forests, hills and delightful river valleys. This is an area with

rather smaller centres of population.

Sweden's capital, Stockholm, starts off with a number of outstanding natural advantages: it lies on 14 islands and has an archipelago of 22,000 islands on one side of it and a beautiful lake on the other. It has a host of attractions ranging from historical sights to entertainment of all kinds. The handsome buildings and the sparkling water add to the beauty of this very fine city.

Each of the counties in the 'lower middle' area of Sweden has

its own particular charm: *Södermanland* with its towns around Lake Mälaren, particularly Mariefred with nearby Gripsholm Castle; *Västmanland*, which was once the centre of the Swedish mining industry and has fascinating towns like Kopparberg, Nora and Sala; and *Uppland* with the cathedral and university town of Uppsala.

To the north lies the folklore county of *Dalarna* which has captivating scenery around Lake Siljan, a justifiably popular holiday area. Towns which deserve a visit include *Leksand*, *Tällberg* and *Mora*.

Beyond Dalarna, Sweden becomes an area of vast forests, tranquil lakes and widening horizons. In *Jämtland* there is some wonderful scenery and the biggest lake in this province is *Storsjön*, on which is the largest town in the area, *Östersund*. To the east lies a long and varied coastline. The High Coast between *Härnösand* and *Örnsköldsvik* is especially charming, while some of the river valleys, stretching into the interior, have splendid scenery – for instance the Ljusnan river valley with the charming little town of *Järvsö*.

You are now entering *Lapland*, a vast area which offers some of the most magnificent scenery in Europe. For example the *Jokkmokk* district covers an area the size of Wales yet has a population of only 7,000 – of which nearly half live in Jokkmokk itself, a town which lies on the Arctic Circle. Not to be missed is *Arjeplog*, on the historic 'Silver Road', also *Gällivare* and *Kiruna*. The latter is the largest town in the far north and has the world's biggest iron ore mine which is also a tourist attraction.

On the coast are the towns of *Umeå*, *Skellefteå* and *Luleå*, while inland northern Lapland stretches to the Finnish and Norwegian borders and embraces superb mountainous scenery.

A PLACE TO STAY

Sweden offers a wide variety of accommodation: luxury hotels, country hotels, motels, summerhouses, youth hostels and camping sites. Self-catering in summerhouses – which may be cottages, chalets or log cabins – is particularly popular. Of benefit to the motorist are the excellent modern motels, many of which have advantageous price deals in summer.

Camping and caravanning are well catered for with nearly 700 approved sites spread across the entire country. There are also some 300 youth hostels at which everyone is welcome – and that includes motorists.

FOOD AND DRINK

There is no lack of opportunity to enjoy good food in Sweden. Like the other Scandinavian countries, fish and seafood feature prominently on the menu and are excellent, while among meat dishes are reindeer and elk. The *Smörgåsbord* is, of course, something of a national institution. It is a mouth-watering help-yourself buffet on a

grand scale to which you can return as frequently as you wish.

Leaving aside the top class restaurants – which provide superlative food – the more modest establishments and cafeterias offer attractive fare at reasonable prices.

The most popular drink is lager which comes in three strengths. Spirits are expensive, while wine is reasonable (depending on what you choose and where you choose it). Off-licence sales are a state monopoly and wines, spirits and strong beer are only available from the *Systembolaget* branches.

INVITING AND CLEAN

Sweden is a well-ordered country and this is immediately apparent from its neat and tidy appearance which also reflects the general affluence of its inhabitants. Swedes live in a country which has a comprehensive and very advanced social welfare system and though they may complain at having to pay for it through high taxation, nevertheless the benefits are there for all to see.

It is a clean country with exemplary standards (which doesn't mean to say you won't come across the odd piece of litter on the ground or graffiti on a wall). Compared to many other countries, Sweden is a peaceful and well-ordered society and this, too, makes life more enjoyable for the visitor.

HELPING THE HANDICAPPED

There are widespread facilities to enable the handicapped to get the maximum enjoyment out of life. Many hotels, restaurants and museums, etc., have facilities for the disabled who are confined to a wheelchair. For those with limited mobility there are special arrangements to enable them to enjoy leisure pursuits. An excellent guide on facilities for the handicapped is available from the Swedish National Tourist Office in London (see Useful Information for address and telephone number).

WEATHER

Sweden has a temperate climate thanks to our old friend the Gulf Stream and the summer weather is broadly similar to that in the UK. There is often less rain and more sunshine than in Britain, but it can be equally capricious and changeable. The summer is, of course, shorter in the north than in the south but central and southern Sweden can be very pleasant in late spring and early autumn.

One advantage of the summer months is the amount of daylight – up to 19 hours out of the 24.

THINGS TO DO AND SEE

Whichever part of the country you choose to visit you will find plenty of things to do and see. There are the traces of Sweden's past: prehistoric rock carvings, Viking burial grounds, splendid castles and manor houses while relics of Sweden's early industrial development have also been well preserved.

The country has some magnificent museums, while open air museums based on collections of old buildings can be found in all areas. At some of these there are demonstrations of old skills and crafts. There has been something of a revival of Swedish folk culture in the last decade and this takes the form of festivals, exhibitions and country markets and they help to preserve Sweden's heritage as well as to entertain. In the north there are interesting museums and collections relating to the history and culture of the Laplanders.

Sweden is very much an outdoor nation and there are many recreational pursuits including canoeing, sailing, trekking, fishing, golfing, swimming, riding and cycling. You can also find more adventurous ways of passing the time like hang-gliding or shooting the rapids in a rubber boat.

Children are well catered for with plenty of activities and amusements to suit all ages.

Also worth mentioning is Sweden's Right of Common Access which gives everybody the right to move freely in the countryside. More details of this law will be found in the chapter on Sports and Recreations.

DRIVE AROUND SWEDEN

Following the success of my first motoring guide, *Drive around Denmark*, I have kept to the same formula with *Drive around Sweden*. The aims are also identical: to provide you with useful, practical information and to lead you to some of the most interesting parts of the country. Use the itineraries but don't feel you must follow them precisely, do some exploring yourself (and if you discover some hidden delights write and tell me about them!).

You will find that Sweden – with a little guidance – grows on you, so relax and enjoy it.

Go and explore at your own pace and if you cover less ground than you planned you can always go back again .... and again. Have a good time!

I would like to acknowledge the help received in the preparation of this book from the Swedish Tourist Board and, in particular from Barbro Hunter and Astrid Ruffhead at the Swedish National Tourist Office in London. I should also like to express my thanks to the staff of the Swedish regional and local tourist offices for their help and to acknowledge the assistance and co-operation received from the UK management and staff of DFDS Seaways. Finally, my thanks to Swedes throughout their pleasant country for their friendly assistance and interest.

GETTING THERE

THE TRADITIONAL shipping route between England and Sweden has always been across the North Sea to Gothenburg. There have been regular sailings for over 100 years and today the tradition is maintained with the DFDS Seaways year round service from Harwich to Gothenburg and summer service from Newcastle to Gothenburg.

The great advantage of taking your car to sea in this way is that you have time to wind down and get in the right frame of mind for your holiday, particularly if you have suffered the all too frequent last-minute pressures before departure. On the return journey you can relax or perhaps prepare yourself for the problems that might be waiting for you!

THE SHIPS

The Harwich – Gothenburg crossing takes 24 hours and is in the hands of two large modern 15,000 ton vessels – 'Tor Scandinavia' and 'Tor Britannia' – which I prefer to call car/cruise liners as they seem so superior to the conventional ferry. Each one takes 1,450 passengers. They are stabilised and air-conditioned and attractively furnished and decorated, with comfortable cabin accommodation. What is more there are berths for all which avoids the unpleasant sight of people pitching camp in the lounges.

As you would expect from Scandinavian ships, they are clean with a well turned out crew. The size and quality of the vessels help to make the crossing an enjoyable part of your holiday. If you are a poor sailor, don't worry, these are big ships and their effective stabilisers combine to reduce motion. If that is not enough, the information office on board has available some effective pills.

The summer-only service from Newcastle to Gothenburg is, at the time of writing, operating twice a week from June to mid-August. The crossing time is 26 – 26½ hours and the ship used on this service is smaller than those on the Harwich route, although it is also air-conditioned and stabilised.

WHAT IS ON BOARD

Facilities on board are comprehensive enough to make the journey a pleasant occasion and they include: lounges, bars, restaurant, cafeteria, shops, two cinemas, disco, sauna and children's playroom.

The spacious restaurant on each ship offers an à la carte menu (which is changed at frequent intervals), a three course table d'hôte set meal and the help-yourself Smörgåsbord. The latter is very good value, particularly if you want to satisfy a substantial appetite. You help yourself and can go back for more, as many times as you like. It is a must if you have ever-hungry children with you. There are all kinds of appetising dishes: fish, seafood, cold meats, cheeses, sweets and several hot dishes. A nice touch is the help-yourself salad bar in the restaurant.

In the morning the restaurant offers a very good help-yourself breakfast at a fixed price and the more you eat the more of a bargain it becomes. A commendable feature is that the bread and rolls are freshly baked on board.

The cafeteria offers both hot dishes and sandwiches, pastries and fruit and a range of beverages. There is usually a dish of the day which is good value. Incidentally, service is included in the cost of meals and drinks in restaurants and bars and you do not need to add anything extra.

Live music for dancing and entertainment is provided in the lounge in the evening, while the disco is generally the haunt of the younger passenger. The two cinemas (for which an entrance charge is made) show first-run films and there are normally two performances each evening. In the morning there is a programme for children.

If you enjoy a pre-dinner drink when you are on holiday it is a good idea to buy your supplies on board rather than pay the high prices for spirits which are charged in Sweden. If you must smoke then the same rule applies to cigarettes and tobacco. On board you can pay for what you eat or drink or buy in the shops in sterling or Swedish kronor or use any of the major credit cards.

The Newcastle – Gothenburg vessel has a slightly reduced range of facilities on board.

CABINS

Cabin accommodation includes single, two-, three- and four-berth cabins (with shower and toilet) or two-, three- and four-berth economy cabins. There is also a de-luxe service called Commodore Class. With this you get a larger cabin with shower and toilet, room service and a free mini-bar; your breakfast is included (and you can have it served in bed if you wish). Fares are based on the accommodation you choose and the date of travel. There are reduced midweek fares called Super-Savers which can cut costs by £45 to £65 on a round trip.

Fares on the Newcastle – Gothenburg service are comparable with those on the Harwich route and mid-week Super-Savers are available while you can also indulge yourself by opting for the more expensive Commodore Class. By contrast the minimum accommodation is a reclining chair.

SAILING TIMES

There are departures three times a week, or alternate days from June to mid-August. Although times are not standardised throughout the year, the usual departure from Harwich is at 11.30, arriving Gothenburg next day at 12.30. From Gothenburg the usual departure time is 15.30 with a next day arrival at Harwich at 14.00. With a car you need to check in one hour before departure.

The terminal at Harwich is at Parkeston Quay and there is now a good road connection from the A12. At Gothenburg ships berth at Skandiahamnen which is across the river from the city of Gothenburg. The signposting to the quay from the principal main roads is good but you should bear in mind that there are other ferry berths at Gothenburg apart from Skandiahamnen, so make sure you follow the right signs. Also traffic around Gothenburg can be heavy so allow yourself plenty of time.

The current schedule from Newcastle has departures at 13.00 or 18.30 (depending on the day of sailing) while the departure times from Gothenburg are 18.30 or 09.30. The check-in time for cars on this route is 1½ hours before departure. You should also remember that the ship does not, in fact, sail from Newcastle but from North Shields. You take the A187 (Howdon Road) near the northern entrance to the Tyne Tunnel and look for the signed right turn to Tyne Commission Quay. Skandiahamnen is used at Gothenburg, as on the Harwich route.

For the south-east of Sweden it is almost as convenient to use the DFDS Seaways service from Harwich or Newcastle to Esbjerg. You then drive across Denmark, finally taking the short ferry crossing to Sweden. You can cross from Helsingør to Helsingborg (25 minutes) or Dragør to Limhamn (50 minutes). One bonus of taking this route is that you can earmark a little time to see Copenhagen. The distance from Esbjerg to Copenhagen is 185 miles but you have to remember that there is a 50-minute ferry crossing, over the Great Belt, midway on your journey.

There are daily sailings from Harwich to Esbjerg throughout the summer (otherwise it is six times a week, apart from mid-winter) while the Newcastle service is three times a week from mid-May to early September at the time of writing.

You can also use one of the shorter sea crossings to the Continent and drive through Belgium or Holland, Germany and Denmark finally crossing by ferry to Sweden. This is, of course, a long and tedious drive which takes the edge off your motoring holiday – especially when you plan to return the same way.

Flying to Gothenburg or Stockholm and renting a car is another alternative but this, like the overland route, eliminates the sea crossing and for me, that is the appropriate way to arrive in Sweden.

MONEY-SAVING PACKAGES

Longship Holidays, the inclusive tour side of DFDS Seaways, provide a comprehensive programme of holidays to Sweden, most of which are for the motorist. These can reduce your costs and, with their go-as-you-please arrangement, your independence is not jeopardized.

The package includes the North Sea crossing and seven hotel cheques, each one covering bed and breakfast at an hotel. There are

117 centres to choose from and at some of them there is higher grade accommodation which requires a supplement. You can also add extra days if you wish. Longship Holidays book you in at the first hotel, and then the latter will make the next reservation for you and so on. The cost of this arrangement (in 1986) is between £213 and £275. There is also a camping go-as-you-please arrangement which is advantageous for those on a budget.

Longship Holidays have a lot of self-catering arrangements in apartments, cabins and summerhouses while other holidays are in country inns and hotels.

REMINDERS

The time used on the ships is Swedish time which can mean that as soon as you get on board you can lose an hour. Access to the car deck is not always permitted during the voyage so when you leave your car take what you need during the crossing. Use an overnight bag so you can avoid toting heavy baggage around. Do not forget to lock your car (doors and boot) and switch off lights if they happen to be on.

If you are going to arrive in Sweden on a Saturday or a Sunday remember that the banks will be closed (this also applies if you arrive on a bank holiday).

DRIVING IN SWEDEN

SWEDEN SHOULD PRESENT few problems to the British motorist and it must be among the easiest European countries in which to drive. There is an excellent and extensive road network, and signposting is good, once you have come to terms with one or two Swedish peculiarities, while parking in the majority of towns and cities presents no great problem.

Traffic on the main highways is not unduly heavy, while on other roads it is extremely light by our standards. Swedish drivers, in my experience, are competent, have reasonably good road discipline and are considerate – especially when you have GB on the back of your car. In short, Sweden should hold no fears for the British motorist and, in fact, it would be a good choice for the first time abroad driver.

Of course you drive on the right, but this is common to all European countries other than Britain and Ireland, and it soon comes naturally. You need to take care starting off first thing in the morning or when you are rejoining a road 'on the wrong side' or are on a deserted road. You also need to 'think right' at roundabouts (of which there are plenty in Sweden) and when positioning yourself for turns.

Overtaking requires more care and this is where a really reliable front seat passenger can be a help.

Some potential visitors are worried about language difficulties but as Sweden uses international road signs this is no problem. There are some specifically Swedish signs but these are largely pictorial and self-explanatory. A few of the words you may come across are given at the end of this chapter. As so many Swedes speak English you should have no difficulties if you get lost or have an emergency of some kind.

One thing which you will need are good maps, particularly if you are following the itineraries in this book. I cannot stress too strongly the importance of good maps which, apart from anything else, can be reassuring when faced with a minor road junction in rural Sweden and with nothing in the vicinity but a few thousand trees.

I use the excellent 1:300,000 scale series published by the Swedish firm of Esselte. There is a total of eight maps in the series which covers the entire country. Apart from keeping you on the right road they include a lot of useful information, while the legend – the key to the various signs and symbols – is in English. Esselte maps are available from the UK distributors McCarta Ltd., 122 Kings Cross Road, London WC1X 9DS. They will also be found at good bookshops who are also map specialists, such as Stanfords at 12 Long Acre, London WC2 9LP.

The Swedish National Tourist Office in London (address and telephone number in the 'Useful Information' chapter) can provide general information on the entire country as well as literature on specific areas and towns. They also have a useful map of Sweden which is fine for planning your visit, but is insufficiently detailed for exploration which involves minor roads.

THE ROAD SYSTEM

One of the most delightful aspects of driving in Sweden is the lack of traffic. There are 50,000 miles of main roads and 700 miles of motorway and on many of these the vehicles are spread very thinly indeed. The main highways, particularly the 'E' roads, do of course carry a considerable weight of traffic, especially in summer and at weekends, but it is rarely excessive. Once away from these roads driving becomes a delightful experience instead of a chore. Incidentally no tolls are levied on any roads or motorways.

In the northern half of the country you can often motor for miles without seeing another vehicle. Around major cities – especially Stockholm and Gothenburg – it can become congested, particularly at rush hour.

Main and secondary roads are well surfaced, while minor roads vary – some are metalled while others have a gravel surface. These unsurfaced roads are perfectly adequate but you need to watch the shoulders and caution should be exercised when they are wet. Resist the temptation to emulate Swedish rally drivers because around the next sharp bend there may well be a huge articulated rig carrying tree trunks. Take care when passing vehicles as loose stones can be thrown up which can hit your windscreen or damage paintwork. In the north the roads can develop humps and dips which is the result of frost heave. There is a warning sign where this has occurred.

The principal highways are the 'E' or European routes. There are seven of them in Sweden and they are:

E3   Gothenburg – Eskilstuna – Stockholm –
        Kappelskär (ferries to Finland).
E4   Malmö – Stockholm – Sundsvall – Umeå –
        Haparanda (Finnish frontier).
E6   Trelleborg (ferry port) – Malmö – Gothenburg –
        Norwegian frontier.
E18   Norwegian frontier – Karlstad – Västerås –
        Stockholm.
E66   Malmö – Kalmar – Norrköping (joins E4 to
        Stockholm and the north).
E75   Norwegian frontier – Östersund – Sundsvall.
E79   Norwegian frontier – Storuman – Lycksele – Umeå.

The Swedish authorities have gone to great lengths to eliminate straightforward road junctions 'on the flat', replacing them either by roundabouts or flyovers. Thus to turn left you very often have to start by turning right and go under or over the road you were on previously.

In the same way the majority of towns and cities have elaborate by-passes to keep non-essential traffic out of the centre. You can drive a long way in Sweden without actually motoring through a town centre. Usually the junctions which give you access to the town are very clearly signed and present no problem. Don't be put off on the approach to a town by the appearance of industrial premises as this can give a misleading impression, press on to the heart of the town and you will probably be pleasantly surprised.

What you are likely to find in town centres are one way streets and pedestrian precincts – so watch out for them. The pedestrianised areas are, of course, extremely pleasant when you want to saunter through a town centre, or window shop. One very useful feature which you will find on the outskirts of many towns is an information panel which displays a street map with key points and approach roads clearly marked. It will be advertised in advance by the international 'i' information symbol and the panel will be located in a lay-by. It will also show the position of the local tourist bureau and this is always a helpful source of information (not the least being the acquisition of a street map).

All main and secondary roads are numbered and this leads me to one important point regarding sign posting. Where you see a sign relating to a specific road number the accompanying place name displayed will be that of the town at the end of this particular road – not the next town or even the one after that. This can, initially, cause a normally calm map reader to panic.

If I have any criticisms of Swedish sign posting it is that sometimes there are too many signs of an equal weight displayed on the same panel which can be difficult to assimilate in a few seconds. At many junctions which are protected by traffic signals there are filter lights so it is important to get into the appropriate traffic lane.

RULES AND REGULATIONS

In Sweden there are four basic speed limits: 50km/h (31 mph), 70km/h (43 mph), 90km/h (56 mph) and 110km/h (68 mph). The last category is normally restricted to motorways. The different limits are clearly signed and there is also a fifth category which is 30km/h (19 mph) which appears in the vicinity of schools and children's play areas. When towing a caravan or a trailer the limit is 70km/h (43 mph) and this applies if the towed vehicle has brakes; if unbraked it is only 40km/h (25 mph). Another rule is that cars towing caravans or trailers must be equipped with extended rear view mirrors and it is regarded as good road manners to move on to the hard shoulder or into a lay-by if traffic has built up behind you.

As already mentioned, the basic rule is drive on the right and overtake on the left. You should give way to traffic approaching from the right unless the road signs indicate to the contrary. Having said that, the law states that no road user has any *absolute* right of way. You must always give way to traffic on a roundabout and you will find that these have lanes marked on them which help the flow of traffic. In one or two cities there are bus lanes which must be avoided while Gothenburg and Norrköping have the added hazard of trams.

At junctions or roundabouts you must give way to pedestrians crossing the road you are entering. When turning left you move across in front of the traffic coming from the opposite direction and turning left, not behind as in the UK. Major junctions frequently have painted 'turn marks' on the road to guide you to your correct position. Traffic lights are often programmed so that turning traffic is controlled independently which can make halts at junctions rather long. The sequence of lights is the same as in the UK.

Another important point, particularly when making a right turn is to watch for cyclists and mopeds. If they are going straight ahead you must give way to them. Cyclists, in Sweden, have the same rights on the road as cars – so keep a sharp eye open for them.

Clear indications should be given when you are turning and, in particular, when you are changing lanes on motorways and main roads. Major cities, such as Stockholm, Gothenburg and Malmö, require special care as urban drivers are less forgiving than those in country areas. Stockholm has some rather involved junctions of which the most confusing is probably Slussen – a multi-level, enclosed circular arrangement which, to make matters worse, was originally designed when traffic drove on the left.

Gothenburg has a traffic system of considerable ingenuity which is aimed at keeping vehicles out of the centre. Even Swedes find it confusing. The city is split into zones which have only one way in and one way out to avoid through traffic using the central area. I have no hesitation in giving it my award for the least sensible traffic system I have ever encountered. But don't let that put you off, it can be cracked and *in extremis* you can always plead ignorance.

When you arrive in Sweden you will find all the cars have their headlights illuminated. The drivers are not forgetful, because it is obligatory, both day and night, to use dipped headlights. It is also illegal to have asymmetric headlights for left-hand driving. These can be adjusted by covering part of the lens with opaque material. I always use black plastic insulating tape – which I cut to cover the appropriate area of the lens and apply to the outer surface of the headlight. You can also buy kits for different makes of cars with the black self-adhesive material marked out to the right shape.

One law that should be strictly obeyed is that referring to drinking and driving. The Swedish law on this subject is one of the toughest in the world and it is rigorously enforced. Police can stop a motorist at any time and require him or her to take a breathalyser test – in other words the random breath test is law in Sweden. You can be prosecuted even if you have only a very low level of alcohol in the blood (50 mg/100 ml) which can be the equivalent of two beers.

There are two degrees of drunken driving, the first of which usually carries a prison sentence while the second involves a fine. In both cases the driver's licence is revoked either for a limited period or absolutely. The moral is clear: don't drink and drive.

In such a safety-conscious country it will come as no surprise that front seat belts must be worn and it is now compulsory for rear seat passengers to wear belts if they are fitted (children under 15 years of age are excluded). Motor cyclists and moped riders must wear crash helmets and this also applies to pillion passengers. Carrying a warning triangle is another statutory requirement.

Should you transgress and break one of the traffic regulations there are fixed fines – using the 'ticket' system – for minor offences. You pay the fine at the post office. There are no on-the-spot fines. Random police checks are quite frequent and in my experience the police are firm but courteous.

Many miles of Swedish roads have one lane in each direction with an additional inside lane marked by a broken white line. This inside lane is, in fact, the hard shoulder and is used by cyclists and pedestrians. But it can be used to allow other vehicles to overtake – this applies particularly if you are a slow moving vehicle such as a car and caravan. It is not, however, an extra traffic lane and must not be used in this way. Nobody is obliged to move onto the shoulder if you are overtaking them, although most people – including truck drivers – do so. If you are on the hard shoulder you must give way to vehicles in the main traffic lane before you move out.

Sweden has an abundance of railway level crossings and although many are protected by automatic barriers there are others which merely have flashing lights. There is always an advance warning sign and a flashing white light merely identifies the position of the crossing. Flashing red lights obviously tell you to stop.

When you take your car to Sweden you will need a valid driving licence (not a provisional one), the certificate of registration and your car should have a GB plate or sticker (the ferry companies provide a sticker with your tickets).

An insurance 'green card' is no longer essential for a vehicle registered in Britain but having one is strongly recommended. Consult your insurance company on this point. It is also worth checking whether you are covered for damage in transit.

Finally, this is really a fair weather motoring guide, as I do not refer to driving in winter. That, as they say, is something else and while the Swedes are used to winter conditions, they pose a more serious problem to the visitor from Britain.

PARKING

Adequate parking facilities are as important as good roads – after all, it is no use travelling if there is nowhere to leave the car when you arrive. Sweden rates a pretty high score in the parking league and although the big city centres can prove to be a problem, elsewhere I have never encountered any difficulty. As you enter a town centre you just need to keep an eye open for the 'P' signs to guide you to car parks, while there is also a considerable amount of street parking allowed.

Parking regulations generally follow international practice but if you are leaving your car in the street overnight – particularly in the suburbs – make sure it is not the night when your side of the street is cleaned and parking is prohibited. A sign will show you which night is bath night.

The sign prohibiting parking is blue with a red border and a red cross; if the sign has just a diagonal red line then you can stop to let someone out of the car or pick them up. A small yellow sign on the same post will show the times when parking is not allowed, but outside these periods you can park. Normally there are three sets of figures, for example:

8 – 17	(Mon – Fri)
8 – 14	(Sat)
8 – 13	(Sun)

The Sunday figures will be in red, the others in black.

Parking meters are quite widespread and valid from 08.00 to 18.00 while the maximum parking time varies but is usually two hours. Charges also vary and are from Skr1 to Skr3 per hour. In Stockholm and Gothenburg the rates will be higher, up to Skr6 in the centre and Skr3 off-centre. However, when you read the chapters on these two cities you will discover how their special tourist cards also entitle you to free parking – a very valuable concession for the visiting motorist.

Some towns also have marked and numbered parking spaces and with these you use a nearby machine to get a parking ticket but you have to punch in the number of your space. At other parks where you pay, you again use a central ticket-issuing machine which is similar to the pay and display type in Britain. One useful feature is that if you put in coins for the maximum parking period, any unexpired time from that day is transferred to the next morning. For example if, at a car park requiring a pay and display ticket from 08.00 to 18.00, you arrive at 17.30 and buy two hours of parking time the ticket will show 09.30 the following day.

Like anywhere else, illegal parking will result in a fine and can result in your car being towed away.

There are multi-storey car parks in the larger towns and cities and charges in these vary – in Stockholm, Gothenburg or Malmö it is likely to be Skr9 – 10 per hour. Some multi-storey parks are attached to stores and you should check how long they are open as they may close quite early in the evening and not reopen until the following morning.

THE FUEL SUPPLY

There are plenty of roadside petrol stations in southern and central

Sweden but they become much less frequent as you motor north. If you are heading for these more distant parts of Sweden my advice is to fill up each morning as a matter of routine. You can also carry a spare can as a reserve, but remember you are not allowed to have petrol in cans on board the ferries.

Virtually all petrol stations are self-service *(Tanka Själv)* and in rural areas they are likely to close at 6.00 p.m. while on main roads they will stay open later. It is worth remembering that a petrol station is often off the main road and you may need to take a slip road to reach it.

Many petrol stations also have pumps which accept Skr10 or Skr100 bank notes and these can be used at any time. Look for the sign *Sedelautomat*. Petrol from these pumps is slightly cheaper. Operation is quite simple, viz:

Insert the desired amount in the appropriate slot.

Push the 'ready' button (green or white).

Select the correct grade if it is a multi-octane rating pump.

Lift the nozzle from the pump, which will start up after a few seconds.

Begin filling in the usual way.

Some pumps have instructions in English as well as Swedish. Filling stations frequently have a pump for diesel fuel – but make sure you don't use it when you really want petrol. Fuel is, of course, sold by the litre and prices at the time of writing are about the same as in the UK. There are three octane ratings: 93, 96 and 98 but 93 octane is being phased out and replaced by lead free petrol because of forthcoming exhaust emission regulations.

BREAKDOWNS AND ACCIDENTS

In the case of a breakdown contact *Larmtjänst*, which is an organisation run by Swedish insurance companies and which has branches all over the country. It operates a 24-hour service and the telephone numbers appear in all the telephone directories (you can also find out the Larmtjänst number at petrol stations or police stations). They charge a fee for their services.

Garages with servicing and repair facilities are usually open from 7.00 a.m. to 5.00 p.m. but are frequently closed at weekends. A 24-hour emergency service is provided in some larger towns. There are also emergency telephones on some major highways.

Should you have the misfortune to have an accident and need the police or an ambulance, dial the emergency number (90000) at the nearest telephone and request the appropriate service: *Ambulans* (ambulance), *Brandkår* (fire brigade) or *Polis* (police). It is not mandatory to call the police in the case of an accident but the driver must give his or her name and address to the other parties involved and may not leave the scene until this has been done. This applies even if the damage may be very slight, while failure to stop after an accident makes the driver liable to a fine or even imprisonment.

DEER, ELK AND REINDEER

These three species, attractive though they may be, constitute a real danger to road users. They have very little road sense and tend to come on to the road without any warning. The reindeer are only found in the north and it is worth bearing in mind that they all belong to the Lapps, so if you kill or injure one you will have to pay compensation for its loss.

Further south (right down to the outskirts of Gothenburg in fact) the real menace is the elk. There has been a population explosion among the elk and although there is an annual cull they are still numerous. They are big – a full-grown elk will weigh up to 800 kg – and one of them hitting your car can do it (and you) a great deal of harm. Dawn and dusk are when they are most active and there are many accidents involving elk. Deer, although not so big, are also to be found in considerable numbers. Many roads now have 'anti-elk' fencing but in any case you should heed the warning road signs and be alert. If you should hit one of these animals you must report it to the police.

CAR SLEEPERS

If you are motoring to northern Sweden you can make your return journey both quick and easy by using the Swedish State Railways' car sleeper services. In summer 1985 they operated twice a week in the peak summer period (July – early August) on three routes: Kiruna – Stockholm, Umeå – Malmö and Luleå – Gothenburg. There is couchette and sleeping car accommodation and a dining car while cars are conveyed in enclosed rail vehicles. Journey times are 18 – 20 hours and fares are reasonable, taking into account the distance and the time that you save.

USEFUL TRANSLATIONS

No entry	*Ej tillträde*
Traffic forbidden	*Förbjuden trafik*
Traffic diversion	*Omläggning av trafik*
Road closed temporarily	*Väg Avstängd*
Exit	*Utfart*
Entrance	*Infart*
Danger	*Fara*
Right	*Höger*
Left	*Vänster*
Drive slowly	*Kör Sakta*
Road works	*Vägarbete*
Loose chippings	*Stenskott*
Warning	*Varning*

Note: if Swedes refer to a mile they mean a metric mile of 10 km which is equal to 6 English miles.

FERRIES

UNLIKE ITS Scandinavian neighbours, Sweden has few internal ferries. Along the west coast there are some short distance ferry links to the adjoining islands. These are only of a few minutes' duration and the fares are, accordingly, quite modest. In one or two cases where the ferry forms the continuation of a road the service is provided by the Ministry of Transport and is free of charge. Services are fairly frequent.

The principal domestic ferry link is between the mainland and the Baltic island of Gotland. There are three routes, the main one being from Nynäshamn, south of Stockholm, to Visby. Crossing time is 5/6 hours and there are one to three sailings a day. Other services are from Oskarshamn to Visby, 4¼/5¼ hours, one to three sailings a day: and Västervik to Visby, 3½ hours, one sailing a day. There is also a summer service of one sailing a day from Grankullavik, on the island of Öland, and Visby, which takes 2 hours 50 minutes. All these services are operated by Rederi AB Gotland.

Although the island of Öland is connected to the mainland by Europe's longest bridge, there is also a ferry connection from Byxelkrok, in the north, to Oskarshamn on the mainland which is also operated by Rederi AB Gotland.

One minor internal ferry service is that from Gränna to the island of Visingsö on Lake Vättern. This takes 20 minutes and there are frequent departures during the day.

Inter-Scandinavian ferry services which are likely to be of interest to the readers of this guide are those running between Denmark and Sweden. The shortest of these is between Helsingør and Helsingborg (25 minutes) and this has an intensive service provided by the Danish State Railways (DSB) with sailings every 15 minutes throughout the day. Scandinavian Ferry Lines run a similar service with up to 50 crossings a day. One point that should be noted is that you cannot pre-book car space on the DSB route and at peak times you may have to wait an hour or more before embarking.

South-east of Copenhagen there is the Scandinavian Ferry Lines' service from Dragør to Limhamn (on the outskirts of Malmö). There are up to 20 sailings a day and the crossing time is 50 minutes. Advance booking is advisable.

From Grenå, on the eastern side of the Danish Jutland peninsula, there are sailings to Varberg (on the Swedish west coast) with 2 – 3 departures a day with the journey taking 3¼/4½ hours. Also from Grenå there is a service 2 – 3 times a day to Helsingborg with a crossing time of four hours.

Further north, on Jutland, Stena Line has an excellent service from Frederikshavn to Gothenburg with up to six sailings a day and a crossing time of 3¼/3½ hours.

Should you be approaching Sweden via Denmark and driving from Esbjerg to either Helsingør or Dragør you will have to cross a stretch of water called the Great Belt *(Storebælt)* which separates the islands of Funen and Zealand. On this 18-mile route there is a frequent service by the Danish State Railways (DSB) using massive car ferries. But because of the volume of traffic, advance booking is most advisable and essential at summer weekends.

Ticket and reservations for this route can be obtained in the UK from DFDS Seaways, who also issue tickets for the DSB Helsingør – Helsingborg, Stena Line Frederikshavn – Gothenburg and SFL Dragør – Limhamn services.

Finally a word of warning: Scandinavian ferry services run with a high degree of efficiency so do make sure that you are ready to drive on board when embarkation begins. Also that when the ship docks you are ready to drive ashore. Turnrounds are short and on the bigger ferries it is a case of getting several hundred vehicles off the ship and a similar number on board in only a few minutes. If it is a multi-car deck ship make sure you remember on which deck you will find your car.

ACCOMMODATION – HOTELS, MOTELS, SUMMERHOUSES, CAMPING

THE RANGE OF accommodation in Sweden is wide, from luxury hotels of the best international standard right down to a simple, inexpensive room. Motorists have the advantage of being completely mobile so they can choose where they want to stay according to their particular requirements and how much they want to spend.

Hotels cover the entire spectrum from plush city centre establishments to modest pensions, while there are many motels which offer an excellent standard of accommodation at a reasonable price. These are usually located on the outskirts of towns or beside main roads. There are also some delightful country hotels in attractive surroundings.

An interesting point is that the low season for hotels is the summer when there are far fewer business customers and no conferences. This is when there are special offers, while at other times of the year special rates only apply at weekends.

As soon as the summer season ends the conference season begins and this continues right round to spring. Conferences seem to be an essential part of the Swedish business scene (and are obviously of vital importance to the hotel industry). Therefore if you travel early or late in the season you may find that a particular hotel is fully booked with conference delegates.

A major aspect of the Swedish holiday accommodation scene is the self-catering dwelling. I say 'dwelling' because it is difficult to put a label on them without the risk of being misleading. They are variously called cottages, cabins, chalets or bungalows but in some cases they may be houses. They range from simple wooden buildings to remarkably lavish houses. I shall keep to cabin, chalet and cottage but when I refer to the latter don't think of English cottages with thatched roofs and roses round the door. There are thousands of these holiday homes in Sweden, many of which are individually owned but available for rent when their owners do not require them. There are also holiday villages and apartments.

As camping is very popular there are plenty of well run sites in attractive locations, while youth hostels are also plentiful. Whatever your choice you may be sure of cleanliness and, at the very least, a reasonable standard of comfort.

The majority of the hotels are included in the Swedish Tourist Board's 'Hotels in Sweden' brochure which is published every year and can be obtained from the Swedish National Tourist Office in London. It also includes details of some of the hotel cheque schemes available and special offers. As Sweden doesn't have a star rating system for hotels, price is really the only guide. The brochure also shows what facilities are available at each hotel.

For accommodation in Stockholm you can use the Tourist Centre in Sweden House, Kungsträdgården or the Hotellcentralen at the Central Station who will make bookings for you. In Gothenburg you will find a similar service at the two city tourist offices at Kungsportsplatsen 2 and Nordstadstorget. In other towns and cities the local tourist information office will help you find the accommodation you require. Even quite small towns and large villages have a tourist office (just look for the familiar 'i' sign) although some of them are only open in the main summer period. They will probably charge a small fee for arranging a booking. Prices are normally inclusive of service and VAT *(Moms)* and most hotels and motels quote on the basis of bed and breakfast.

You can expect to pay more in Stockholm for hotel rooms but there are useful savings to be made by staying on the outskirts of the capital. You can then use the metro system to reach the city centre and this is particularly useful if you wish to avoid driving into the heart of the capital.

As already mentioned, the best deals at hotels are to be found in summer and another benefit is the family rate which can be an inclusive price for two adults and one or two children all sharing the same bedroom.

Major hotels and many motels have all rooms with private bath or shower, telephone, radio and TV. They often have other facilities such as an exercise room, sauna and swimming pool.

The top quality hotels provide a very high level of comfort and cuisine, while motels, especially those of recent construction, have high standards and reasonable prices.

COUNTRY HOTELS

Of particular charm are the country hotels some of which are very old-established while others may be former manor houses or farmhouses. Invariably they enjoy beautiful surroundings, perhaps with a lake and spacious grounds, and many of them provide a range of activities and recreations. Quite a few are renowned for the excellence of their cuisine and some specialise in local and regional delicacies.

Most country hotels are independently owned and 30 of them have formed an association called Countryside Hotels. Not all of them, in my opinion, qualify for this title and they do vary in both size and price. I have visited quite a number and the best are featured in the itineraries in this book.

There are also mountain hotels which offer excellent facilities and accommodation in more remote locations. These make an ideal base if you want to explore a particular area.

HOTEL GROUPS AND HOTEL CHEQUES

There are several well-established Swedish hotel groups and also associations of independent hotels and there are a variety of hotel cheque schemes which can be particularly advantageous to the motorist. Here are details of the main ones with some idea of their size and scope.

Sara Hotels Thirty hotels in towns and cities from Gothenburg on the west coast to Riksgränsen in the north. Modern and well furnished and mostly in town locations. During the summer they have a special rate for holders of the Scandinavian Bonus Pass. At the time of writing the cost per person for bed and breakfast is Skr140. The Pass offers hotel discounts in all the Nordic countries and costs £10 and is available from selected travel agents and also Sara Hotel Service. Incidentally no charge is made for children under 15 years' old who share their parents' room and they get breakfast at half price.

Scandic A major chain of over 50 motels and hotels. They offer a very acceptable standard of accommodation and their latest additions are excellent. During the summer (5 May – 11 Sept) you can stay at bargain rates on any day of the week using Scandic Cheques. Bed and breakfast per person in a double room using the cheques costs Skr170. Outside the summer season the cheques are only valid at weekends but they cost only Skr145 for bed and breakfast. Children under 15 years of age are free if they share the parents' room. The breakfast charge for a child is Skr20. All rooms have bath or shower, telephone, radio and colour TV. They also have rooms for non-smokers (quite common in Sweden). Many of Scandic's motels have a pool, solarium, sauna and gymnasium. They have now embarked on a new chain of town centre hotels called Scandic Crown, and also highway inns called Scandic Vägkrog.

Inter-S Hotels Thirty independent hotels, the majority in town centre locations. Some are old-established but the interiors have invariably been refurbished and brought up to a high standard. They offer summer prices from Skr140 per person in a double room, including breakfast. Up to two children under 15 can share their parents' room without charge. With the Inter-S Hotels Holiday Pass you can stay five nights but only pay for four. The Pass is available free of charge from any Inter-S hotel and is also valid at over 70 hotels in Denmark, Norway and Finland.

Reso Hotels A group of 20 hotels in both town and resort locations stretching from Nya Hotel Tylösand on the west coast to the Hotel Ferrum in Kiruna in Lapland.

Sweden Hotels A very wide selection of over 130 independently-owned hotels all over Sweden. They include city hotels, tourist hotels, inns, conference hotels and boarding houses. There are special family terms in three different price categories in summer. In 1985 a room with breakfast for two adults and two children (under 18) any weekend 20 June – 5 August cost from Skr280 to Skr420.

Biltur-Logi This is a hotel cheque scheme which offers bed and breakfast at over 200 budget-priced hotels, pensions and inns *(Värdshus)*. You pay for a 'Hotel Passport' which includes a handbook, road map and details of all the participants. The price per person, in a double room, depends on the category of the hotel. The 1985 prices were: Budget Skr79, Good Value Skr98 and Comfortable Skr118. Breakfast is extra (usually Skr25–30). Many hotels offer the Biltur-Logi terms for most if not all the year. The Hotel Passport can be obtained from Mrs. B. Wager, 38 Loosens Drive, Woodlands Park, Maidenhead, Berks. SL6 3UT and costs £4.00.

Swed-Cheque This is a major hotel cheque scheme which is valid at Sara, Inter-S, SAS and Sweden Hotels. Nearly 200 hotels are included and there are two price groups: Budget Skr130 and Quality Skr180. This is the price per person including the usual lavish buffet breakfast. Budget rooms will normally have washing facilities while Quality rooms will include a private shower and toilet. The cheques are valid 1 June – 1 September.

SELF-CATERING

As I have already mentioned there is a vast number of self-catering dwellings available for rent. Some can be very much away from it all and on their own while others are in groups, centres or villages.

Purpose-built chalets or cottages usually consist of a living room, two or three bedrooms, a well-equipped kitchen, bathroom and toilet. Most accommodate up to six persons and are provided with cooking utensils, cutlery, blankets and pillows. Visitors have only to supply sheets and towels.

The cabins tend to be less sophisticated and to be sited in more remote areas. Kitchen equipment, blankets and pillows are normally included.

There are also about 250 chalet villages which offer additional amenities which can include such things as a grocery or general store while the more elaborate may have a leisure centre with a restaurant, swimming pool, sauna, launderette and a playground. There may also be recreations such as mini-golf, tennis, riding, fishing and possibly boat or bicycle rental.

Different tourist regions produce their own brochures which describe and illustrate the cottages and cabins in their areas. As an example the 24-page Västergötland brochure features over 200 properties plus two holiday villages. Cottages, etc. are given a one to five star rating and a typical three star cottage is Skr940 per week, while a five star chalet is Skr1,420 a week. The charges at a holiday village, overlooking a lake with bathing and other facilities within walking distance, are from Skr1,680 to Skr2,180 a week.

There are also flats in modern blocks and apartments which might suit those who prefer to remain in urban surroundings.

Apart from the cottages, chalets, cabins and flats which are organised for letting there are many more which are available on a casual basis. Look for the sign 'Stuga' (it means cottage) beside the road and this will indicate that someone has one or more cottages to let.

FARMHOUSES AND ROOMS

A number of farms in Sweden offer accommodation, either in the main farmhouse or in an adjoining cottage. The total is not great compared with, for example, Denmark where farmhouse holidays are highly developed and organised. On Swedish farms rooms are usually offered on a bed and breakfast basis with self-catering facilities provided for cooking other meals. This accommodation can be booked through a local tourist office and the typical price range is Skr75 to Skr150 per person per day. A list of farmhouse accommodation is available from Land-Resor, Vasagatan 12, S-105 33 Stockholm.

For other budget-priced overnight accommodation look for a 'Rum' sign as you drive along. 'Rum' simply means room and that is exactly what you get – a room without breakfast. Prices are very reasonable but they vary from place to place. In 1985 they averaged Skr70-75 per night.

YOUTH HOSTELS

There are some 300 youth hostels (called *Vandrarhem*) in Sweden and they come in a variety of guises from former mansions and castles to modern buildings and they even include a renovated sailing ship, the 'Af Chapman' which is moored in Stockholm harbour. Most of them have two- and four-bedded rooms or family rooms and have self-catering facilities. Meals or light refreshments can be obtained at some of them.

They are run by the Swedish Touring Club (STF) and if you are a member of the YHA you will pay Skr33-44 a night, while non-members are charged an additonal Skr15. You are expected to provide your own sheet sleeping bag of approved model and size (other types are not allowed).

There are no restrictions on motorists using the hostels and while some are open all year round others are restricted to summer-time only. In the peak summer months it is advisable to book in advance. A complete guide to all the hostels is available from the STF, Box 25, S-101 20 Stockholm, price approx. Skr25. Unfortunately it is not available in the UK nor does it have any English translation, but the hostels are illustrated and a small map showing the location of each one is provided. The hostels are also listed in the International Youth Hostel Handbook, Volume 1, available from the Youth Hostels Association, price £2.95.

The STF also run several mountain centres in northern Sweden and are responsible for the mountain huts along the long-distance footpaths. They also publish a list of guest harbours and offer guidance to walkers and canoeing enthusiasts.

CAMPING AND CARAVANNING

Camping and caravanning holidays are tremendously popular in Sweden and this is reflected in the number of sites to be found all

over the country. There are around 680 officially approved sites and they are classified with one, two or three stars depending on the facilities provided, as follows.

One star site: daily inspection, drinking water, WC's, washing facilities, hot water for dishwashing, laundering and showers, garbage bins.

Two star site: as for a one star site plus caravan drainage, electricity for shavers, kiosk, foodstuffs, telephone and electric sockets for caravans.

Three star site: in addition to two star site facilities it includes 24 hour inspection, reception, postal service, tourist information, cafeteria, cooking facilities, play and recreational activities, assembly room and car wash.

Many sites offer additional facilities which can extend from boat rental to riding. The majority of sites are open from 1 June – 1 September while a considerable number are also open in April and May. About 180 sites remain open all year round and about the same number offer special facilities for the disabled.

The cost for one night for a family with a tent or caravan is approximately Skr30-50. A camping card is required and this will be issued at the first site you visit and will cost the equivalent of about £1.50, and it is then valid for the entire season. The card is not required if you have an International Camping Carnet.

An alternative to having a tent or caravan is to rent one of the 4,200 camping cabins which are available at 350 sites. They have between two and six beds and cooking facilities and utensils but no bed clothes. You can of course use any of the site facilities and the cost of a four-bed cabin is in the region of Skr100-200 per night. A few of these on-site cabins I have seen are on the rough and ready side and are not very attractively located, but others look acceptable enough and have been more imaginatively sited.

It must be said that some of the larger and more popular sites in peak summer are both very crowded and have a somewhat frenetic atmosphere. By contrast there are plenty of sites, including a lot of the smaller ones, which occupy simply superb locations, often beside a river, lake or the sea.

Camping cheques, valid at over 350 sites, can be bought before your holiday as part of a travel package from Watling Travel, 63 Watling Avenue, Edgware, Middx. HA8 0LD. Longship Holidays (see 'Useful Information') also offer camping cheque holidays with a choice of 20 carefully selected sites.

A detailed guide to approved sites is in the annual *Camping Sverige* handbook which is available from bookshops and larger camping sites in Sweden or can be obtained from Stanfords, 12 Long Acre, London WC2 9LP, price £5.95. The handbook is in Swedish but with key information and symbols translated into English. The Swedish National Tourist Office in London has an abbreviated list of camping sites which is available on request.

*on board one of the ships of DFDS Seaways.
ke cruise liners than the usual concept of a*

*ther sort. The 1892 steamer 'Trafik' has
on Lake Vättern from the resort of Hjo.*

31

It should be mentioned that butane gas such as Camping Gaz is not available in Sweden. Only propane gas called Gasol is obtainable. Therefore it is advisable to take your own supplies of butane gas with you.

FACILITIES FOR THE HANDICAPPED

Sweden is in the forefront of the European countries catering for the needs of the handicapped. It is therefore worth mentioning that many hotels, motels, self-catering centres and camping sites have facilities for the handicapped. A lot of hotels in Sweden not only have rooms designed for the disabled but also for those who suffer from allergies. A helpful guide for the disabled visitor is available from the Swedish National Tourist Office in London.

Swedish Hotel Cheques are obtainable from the Norwegian State Railways Travel Bureau, 21-24 Cockspur Street, London SW1Y 2DB; Scantours, 8 Spring Gardens, Trafalgar Square, London SW1A 2BG; and Swedish Chalets, 28 Hillcrest Road, Orpington, Kent BR6 9AW. Scandic Cheques are available from Swedish Chalets while the Scandinavian Bonus Pass is obtainable from the Norwegian State Railways Travel Bureau.

All prices quoted are correct at the time of writing but are, of course, subject to alteration.

ABOVE – M.S. 'I
by DFDS Seaways
via Harwich-Goth

BELOW – The fer
to make the cross

ABOVE – Another view
These vessels are more
ferry.

BELOW – A ship of and
regular summer sailing

Typical scenery: forested hills, farmland and water – in this case the broad, gently flowing Klarälven in Värmland.

ABOVE – Sweden has some fine castles and one of the most impressive is at Läckö, where it enjoys a beautiful position on Lake Vänern.

BELOW – With its thousands of lakes Sweden offers unlimited opportunities for canoeing, sailing and bathing. This scene is near Växjö.

FOOD AND DRINK

THERE IS NO DOUBT that Swedish food has perked up considerably in recent years. A new generation of chefs with enterprising and innovative ideas has emerged. At the same time the best of Sweden's national dishes have been retained while there has been a resurgence of interest in the older traditional recipes and regional delicacies. Many restaurants are now serving *Husmanskost* (literally home cooking) and more and more of them are using produce found in their own particular areas.

Nouvelle cuisine has appeared and too often this seems to be slavishly following fashionable trends without adding much to one's enjoyment of the food (unless you consider that the addition of kiwi fruit to every dish is a good thing).

Fish forms the basis of much that is best in Swedish cuisine while there is a strong emphasis on the use of really fresh, high quality raw materials.

When I was researching this book, food obviously figured prominently – as it is one of the principal pleasures of a holiday abroad. I ate in a very wide variety of establishments from renowned (and expensive) restaurants all the way down the scale to small roadside cafeterias. I never had anything that was really disappointing and I did have many highly enjoyable meals. I was particularly impressed by the enthusiasm of the restaurateurs and their staff.

If you think that Sweden's only catering accomplishment is their *Smörgåsbord*, you will, I feel sure, be due for a very pleasant surprise.

THE SMÖRGÅSBORD

The Smörgåsbord is probably the one Swedish culinary achievement which is widely known beyond the country's borders. Basically it is a lavish help-yourself buffet featuring a gorgeous mouthwatering selection of fish, meat, salads, relishes, hot dishes, cheeses and desserts. You pay a fixed price and eat as much as you like. The price depends to some extent on the restaurant and where it is located and also the range of dishes available. It averages Skr80 to Skr95, but at weekends some hotels and restaurants feature a more elaborate version which may cost considerably more, say Skr150 to Skr170. The Smörgåsbord is usually available at lunch time and is much less likely to be offered in the evening. The idea of the Smörgåsbord originated in the 18th century when it was really a selection of appetisers that were consumed before sitting down to the main meal. It gradually became more elaborate and then finally replaced the main meal itself.

An essential of the Smörgåsbord is herring (in various guises) which is where you start and then continue with egg and other fish, meat, salads and hot dishes finishing with cheese and the dessert – which is frequently a refreshing fruit salad. Among the dishes you are likely to find are smoked eel, dill-cured salmon, smoked salmon, prawns or shrimps, pâtés, ham, tongue, beef and perhaps smoked reindeer. The hot dishes will probably include meatballs, sausages, chicken and omelettes with a choice of fillings.

The idea is not to pile your plate with a glorious mixture but to make several trips to the Smörgåsbord. Little and often should be your motto.

Many restaurants now offer a mini-Smörgåsbord called *Smör, ost och sill* (butter, cheese and herring). This will probably be a plate of herring, with bread and butter and cheese.

You drink beer with the Smörgåsbord, with perhaps an aquavit to start you off, and coffee to complete the meal. (But don't forget the drink and drive law if this is just a mid-day stop on your journey).

BREAKFAST

The help-yourself buffet-style breakfast is virtually universal throughout Sweden. Some of these breakfast buffets offer a bewildering variety of dishes which are likely to tempt even those who normally start the day on nothing more than a cup of coffee.

The usual spread includes fruit juice and milk, cereal and oatmeal (or a muesli), a variety of bread and rolls, jam, marmalade, cheese, boiled eggs, cold meat and tea and coffee. You will often find also herring, fish pâté or roe, and even porridge. Eggs may be in two containers – each one marked with the number of minutes the eggs have been boiled or else 'soft' and 'hard'. Bread can include some sweet varieties and you often have a toaster for making your own toast.

Finally, when you select the milk jug just be warned that one will frequently contain sour milk *(filmjölk)*. The Swedes like it, but visitors may not find it very enjoyable.

SOME SWEDISH DISHES

As already mentioned, the basis of Swedish cuisine is fish and this includes halibut, turbot, shrimps, prawns, lobster but above all herring and salmon. Baltic herring is a very old established staple of the Swedish diet. Fresh grilled Baltic herring are wonderful, particularly when eaten in some outdoor restaurant beside the sea.

Gravad lax – dill-cured salmon – is a great Swedish speciality which shouldn't be missed while salmon is also available fresh or lightly smoked. Another alternative is Lax Pudding, which is salmon with potato and egg with melted butter. Crayfish is another Swedish delicacy for which 8 August marks the beginning of the season when it appears on restaurant menus and when many people hold crayfish parties. Unfortunately there are no longer enough local crayfish to go round and most of them have to be imported.

Among freshwater fish are trout and Arctic Char *(Röding)*. This is somewhat similar to salmon trout and is delicious. The latter are only found in the north or in Lake Vättern.

Meat dishes may include beef, lamb, pork or veal while you are almost sure to be offered either elk or reindeer (the latter appears on almost all menus in the north). Elk is on the gamey side, but both are very enjoyable while smoked reindeer is very good. You can also try *Pytt-i-Panna*, a Swedish hash, which if it is well prepared is splendid. There are numerous varieties of sausages, some of which are almost a meal in themselves. For instance *Isterband* sausages include beef, pork, potato, barley, onion and spices. There are also some very good smoked sausages and very tasty meatballs *(Köttbullar)*.

Salads and vegetables are good and the wild mushrooms *(Murkla* and *Chanterelle)* are worth trying. The Swedes also make good use of the wild berries which are to be found in such profusion. They include lingon berries (cranberries), which accompany meat dishes, or are used as a dessert, and also made into drinks and jam. Another one is *Hjortron*, which are yellow cloudberries and these are very nice as a dessert with ice cream. The latter is excellent and at some restaurants ice cream is a help-yourself dessert. You go to the cold cabinet and select what you want from a whole range of flavours. If you have children this will prove especially popular.

Cheeses include *Herrgårdost*, a hard cheese; *Grevé*, which is a Swedish Emmentaler; *Västerbotten*, rich and strong; and *Kryddost*, which is spiced with caraway and cloves.

Bread includes the *Knäckebröd*, which is a dry crispbread, and also *Tunnbröd*. This looks like a very thin crisp pancake. Newly baked it is soft and can be rolled up and filled with, for example, smoked reindeer.

Among cakes baked to traditional recipes are Swedish applecake and curd cake *(Ostkaka)* which is served with cottage cheese. *Spettekaka*, a pyramid cake, baked on a spit, is also very enjoyable while if you are visiting one of the folk or outdoor museums you are very likely to find on offer fresh waffles with jam and cream. With a good cup of coffee this makes an enjoyable and inexpensive snack. Coffee, incidentally, is excellent and available everywhere because, along with the Finns, the Swedes drink more of it per head than any other nation. I am sure that without coffee Sweden would very quickly come to a standstill.

WHERE TO EAT AND DRINK

Places to eat and drink fall into different categories. Here are some of them:

Bar	Snacks and light meals. Do not necessarily sell any kind of alcohol.
Bistro	Can be a place for inexpensive meals but there are also some upmarket restaurants which call themselves bistros.

FOOD AND DRINK

Café	Cakes and coffee, also sandwiches and salads and sometimes light meals.
Cafeteria	Self-service establishments which may be quite simple, offering only sandwiches and snacks, or more elaborate with a range of hot dishes.
Hotel	Hotel restaurants generally cover all meals from breakfast to dinner.
Konditori	The place for cakes and coffee.
Korvkiosk	Normally open late and offering fast food items such as hot dogs, hamburgers and grilled chicken. Something of a Swedish institution.
Motel	Usually has a cafeteria with a good range of dishes and quite frequently it will have a restaurant as well.
Restaurant	Wide range of food and drinks.
Wärdshus	The traditional Swedish word for inn (modern spelling: *Värdshus*). Now they are more frequently restaurants and quite often they have a high standard of cuisine with prices to match.

Besides establishments in the above categories there are plenty of speciality restaurants – such as pizzerias and Chinese restaurants and a growing number of fast food outlets. The latter include such familiar names as Wimpy and McDonald.

Opening hours vary but, in general, restaurants are open from 11.30 a.m. to midnight (last orders for hot dishes may be somewhat earlier – 9.00 p.m. or 10.00 p.m.).

Like anywhere else, the best restaurants are expensive. For example, a very good Stockholm restaurant charges Skr245 for their four course table d'hôte dinner while another one has a gourmet menu at Skr280. Further down the scale, at a good restaurant the cost of a three course dinner will be Skr175 to Skr190, while a bottle of house wine will be Skr75. Smaller establishments will feed you very well for less while a cafeteria will bring the price down even more.

Lunches can be something of a bargain as very many restaurants offer special fixed price meals at Skr25 to Skr35. You will have a choice of two or three dishes and with the one you select there will be bread and butter, a salad and probably a cup of coffee. Some also include a soft drink or milk. These prices even apply in the cities and I have enjoyed an excellent Skr35 lunch in the heart of Stockholm while the cheapest I tried was Skr18.50 which was a very good fish pie and a salad. Coffee was extra, but at Skr2 a cup who could complain?

Incidentally, at most restaurants and cafés you can have a second cup of coffee without charge. Coffee and a slice of mouth-watering gateau will be Skr20 to Skr30.

If you want to economise go to a Korvkiosk where you will get a grilled sausage and chips for Skr14. If you want a break while driving there are cafeterias along the main roads, some being part of petrol station chains such as Gulf and OK. Others include Checkers and Scandic. They are always very clean and the food appetising.

DRINKS

The main domestically-produced drink in Sweden is a lager-type beer which comes in three strengths: *Lättöl* (class I), a light beer, then the so-called *folköl* (class II) which is stronger, and *starköl* (class III) which is the strongest. Popular brands are *Pripps Blå* and *Falcon*. Classes I and II are sold in supermarkets but class III is only available from the state monopoly off-licences.

Vodka and aquavit *(snaps)* have been traditional Swedish drinks for a very long time. The most popular brand of vodka is *Absolut*. Aquavit is available in a variety of brands, the leading one being *Skåne Aquavit*. Some of them are flavoured, such as *Svart Vinbärs Brannvin* which is aquavit with blackcurrants. Both vodka and aquavit are served neat and well chilled.

Another Swedish drink is *Punsch* which can be served well chilled after dinner with the coffee or it may be served hot with, for example, the traditional yellow pea soup. It includes pure alcohol, arrak and sugar so you have been warned.

There are also some liqueurs, such as the one available in the north which is made from lingon berries.

Wines are all imported and a house wine in a restaurant will cost Skr70 to Skr80 a bottle. Better quality wines go up in price accordingly. You can often get a carafe or glass of wine and the house wines, in my experience, have always been very drinkable. Red is *rött*, white is *vitt* and rosé is the same. Dry is *torrt* and sweet is *sött*.

Spirits are expensive – a gin and tonic or whisky will be around Skr45 in an hotel or restaurant.

Wines, spirits and strong beer are only sold through the state-owned *Systembolaget* shops which have a monopoly. They are only open Mondays – Fridays from 9.00 a.m. to 6.00 p.m. An inexpensive bottle of table wine will cost from Skr25 at Systembolaget. Incidentally the state-owned shops stock a very fine selection of wines, especially those in the bigger towns. The minimum age for buying alcoholic beverages is 20.

Finally, don't forget the drink and drive laws; even a little alcohol will put you over the limit.

USEFUL TRANSLATIONS

Non-alcoholic drinks

Apelsin juice	orange juice
Citron	lemon
Choklad	chocolate

FOOD AND DRINK

Frukt juice	fruit juice
Kaffe	coffee
Läskedryck	fizzy drinks
Mineralvatten	mineral water
Mjölk	milk
Filmjölk	sour milk
Lattmjölk	low fat milk
Saft	fruit squash
Sodavatten	soda water
Te	tea
Tomatjuice	tomato juice
Vatten	water

Menu terms

Barnmatsedal	children's menu
Dagens rätt	dish of the day
Drycker	drinks
Efterrätt	dessert
Filé	fillet (meat or fish)
Fisk	fish
Friterad	deep fried
Frukost	breakfast
Frukt	fruit
Fylld	stuffed
Förrätt	hors-d'œuvre/starter
Grillad	grilled
Grönsaker	vegetables
Halstrad	grilled
Huvudrätt	main dish
Kall	cold
Kokt	boiled
Kött	meat
Lunch	lunch
Middag	dinner
Ost	cheese
Ostbricka	cheese board
Pocherad	poached
Rökt	smoked
Sallad	salad
Smörfräst	sautéed
Smörgåsbord	help-yourself buffet
Soppa	soup
Stekt	fried
Varm	hot
Ångkokt	steamed

Food terms – fish and shellfish

Ansjovis	anchovy

42

Blåmussla	mussels
Böckling	smoked herring
Fiskbullar	fish balls
Flundra	flat fish
Forell	trout
Gravad lax	marinated salmon
Helgeflundra	halibut
Hummer	lobster
Krabba	crab
Kräffor	crayfish
Lax	salmon
Makrill	mackerel
Ostron	oyster
Rom	roe
Räkor	shrimps/prawns
Röding	Arctic char
Rödspätta	plaice
Rökt lax	smoked salmon
Sill	herring
Inlagd sill	marinated herring
Skaldjur	shellfish
Sjötunga	sole
Strömming	Baltic herring
Torsk	cod
Ål	eel

Meat

Biff	beefsteak
Fläskkarré	loin of pork
Fläsk	pork
Fläskstek	roast pork
Grillkorv	hot dog
Kalvfilé	fillet of veal
Kalvkött	veal
Korv	sausage
Kotlett	chop/cutlet
Köttbullar	meat balls
Lammkotletter	lamb chops
Lammkött	lamb
Lammsadel	saddle of lamb
Lever	liver
Leverpastej	liver paste
Oxkött	beef
Oxfilé	fillet of beef
Oxstek	roast beef
Revbensspjäll	spare ribs
Rökt kött	smoked meat
Skinka	ham
Wienerkorv	frankfurters

FOOD AND DRINK

Poultry and game

Anka	duck
Fasan	pheasant
Gås	goose
Kyckling	chicken
Rapphöna	partridge
Renkott	reindeer meat
Vilt	game
Älg	elk

Cheese, eggs and cream

Grädde	cream
Vispad grädde	whipped cream
Gräddfil	sour cream
Omelett	omelette
Ost	cheese
Ägg	egg
Ägg, löskokt	soft boiled egg
Ägg, hårdkokt	hard boiled egg
Ägg, stekt	fried egg
Äggröra	scrambled egg

Vegetables

Blandade grönsaker	mixed vegetables
Blomkål	cauliflower
Brysselkål	Brussels sprouts
Bönor	beans
Grönkål	kale
Gurka	cucumber
Lök	onion
Morötter	carrots
Murkla	morel mushrooms
Persilja	parsley
Pommes frites	French fries/chips
Potatis	potatoes
Potatismos	mashed potato
Rödkål	red cabbage
Sparris	asparagus
Spenat	spinach
Svamp	mushroom
Vitkål	white cabbage
Ärter	peas

Fruit

Ananas	pineapple
Apelsin	orange
Banan	banana
Blåbär	bilberry

Citron	lemon
Hallon	raspberry
Hjortron	cloudberry
Jordgubbe	strawberry
Lingon	cranberry
Nöt	nut
Persika	peach
Päron	pear
Vindruvor	grape
Äpple	apple

Various

Bakverk	pastries
Bröd	bread
Franskbröd	French bread
Glass	ice cream
Kaka	cake
Kex	biscuits
Knäckebröd	crispbread
Marmelad	marmalade
Mörkt rågbröd	rye bread
Pankaka	pancake
Ris	rice
Rostat bröd	toast
Smör	butter
Smörgås	sandwich
Socker	sugar
Sylt	jam
Tunnbröd	thin barley bread
Våffla	waffle

Selected dishes

Bruna Bönor Baked brown beans flavoured with vinegar and served with pork, meatballs or sausage.

Färsk Potatis New potatoes with herring, sour cream and spring onions.

Janssons Frestelse Mr. Janssons's temptation. Layers of anchovies, sliced potatoes and onions baked in cream.

Pytt-i-Panna Diced meat, fried potatoes, served with a fried egg and pickled beetroot.

Sillbricka A variety of herring dishes.

Ärtsoppa Yellow pea soup with pork and traditionally served on Thursdays.

Sjömansbiff Sailor's stew prepared with beef, onions and potatoes and cooked in beer.

ATTRACTIONS FOR CHILDREN AND ADULTS

THERE IS no shortage of things to see and do in Sweden. High on the list of attractions is one that is there in abundance and which is completely free: the scenery. The varied and lengthy coastline, often fringed with small islands, the forests, the countless lakes and the countryside – ranging from gentle meadows in the south to the vast impressive wilderness in the north – provide a constant source of enjoyment. Sweden's unique Right of Common Access (to quote its formal title) allows you to move freely in the countryside and adds to your pleasure.

The Swedes have also paid great attention to their history and heritage and this is reflected in the many relics of the past which have been carefully preserved. They range from Bronze Age rock carvings to the open air museums with collections of old buildings which provide a fascinating glimpse of a previous age.

Not to be overlooked are the local community and historical centres – called *hembygdsgård* (and often a good place for home-made cakes, waffles and coffee!). There is also a growing number of centres where you can watch handicrafts being made and old skills performed bringing the past very much to life.

Museums are there in plenty and cover a vast range of subjects (there are at least 50 museums in Stockholm alone). Often a great deal of imagination has been shown in the way the exhibits have been assembled and displayed which increases their interest and appeal. They are a far cry from the usual concept of a museum.

Castles and manor houses will also be found, invariably enjoying beautiful locations which add to their historic or architectural interest.

In the introduction to a recent Swedish Tourist Board publication, HM King Carl XVI Gustaf mentioned that Swedes have a soft spot for children and that, as a result, there are special activities and attractions for the younger generation. This is certainly true and there are many things that will appeal to children, whether they are the more organised ones, like the amusement and activity parks or really simple ones, like a sandy beach.

The activity parks, called *Sommarland*, are well worth a family visit. You pay an admission fee and then all (or nearly all) of the attractions within the park are free and can be enjoyed any number of times. They include all sorts of things: boats, canoes, trampolines, pony rides, aerial cableways, rides, water chutes – the biggest centre has over 70 different activities for the young visitor to enjoy. They make a marvellous day out for the family even if they are not quite as much fun for adults.

Then there are the thrilling rides in the Liseberg amusement park in Gothenburg or at Stockholm's Gröna Lund Tivoli, Kolmården's wonderful zoo and safari park, Father Christmas's world near Mora and the enormous wild west complex at High Chaparral and a whole lot more. The King was quite right.

Of course, there are other attractions which can be enjoyed

equally well by adults and children, like riding a veteran steam train or panning for gold (the real thing!) or going to see the seals on a seal safari.

My list of attractions is broad but by no means includes all that Sweden has to offer. In most cases I have given an indication of opening times but I should emphasise that some places open for a comparatively short summer season. At other times they may have restricted opening hours or be closed. (You can always check with the Swedish National Tourist Office in London or, better still, visit the local tourist office).

Expect to pay an entrance fee at most museums, etc. Parking is usually free. Most places have some catering facilities and these are invariably clean and inviting (and quite often very good value).

The various attractions are listed by the Swedish counties or provinces. Those marked with a ☆ should be of interest to children, while the numbers identify the attractions on the accompanying map.

SKÅNE

1 Helsingborg Medieval Keep *(Kärnan)* above the town provides good views across the Sound to Denmark. OPEN DAILY IN SUMMER. Town Museum. OPEN DAILY MAY – AUG AND DAILY EXCEPT MON SEPT – APR. Royal summer palace – Sofiero. PARK OPEN DAILY MAY – MID SEPT.

2 Båstad Holiday resort with picturesque streets and houses and attractive beaches nearby. The 'tennis town' of Sweden.

3 Klippan Silver Hill Aircraft and Motor Museum Large collection of Rolls-Royce cars and also Lipizzaner horses. ☆ (On road 21). OPEN DAILY MAY – SEPT. Museum railway, Klippan-Ljungbyhed. ☆ OPERATES SUN JUNE – AUG.

4 Landskrona Impressive 16th century citadel, one of Scandinavia's best preserved fortifications. OPEN IN SUMMER.

5 Malmö Third largest city. Malmöhus Castle. Museum covers city's history from the Middle Ages to the present day. Also Technical and Transport Museum. House of the Commandant houses a military collection. ALL OPEN DAILY, EXCEPT MON. Hyllie water tower 253 ft above sea level, offers splendid views. OPEN DAILY, (NOT SAT, 15 SEPT – 15 MAY).

6 Lund Town founded by King Canute in 1020. Cathedral, regarded as the finest Romanesque building in Scandinavia, was consecrated in 1145. Inside is the fascinating 14th century astronomical clock. *Kulturhistoriska Museet* or *Kulturen*. ☆ Interesting collection of old buildings plus fine collections of china, glass, silverware and textiles. OPEN DAILY. Museum of Art and Museum of Classical Antiquities. OPEN DAILY EXCEPT SAT.

7 Bosjökloster Castle and former Benedictine convent founded in 1080. OPEN MAY – OCT. (On road 23).

8 Skånes Djurpark, Höör ☆ Animal park with about 400 Scandinavian animals. Also reconstruction of a prehistoric village. Surrounded by a large recreation area, *Frostavallen*. OPEN DAILY IN SUMMER.

9 Kristianstad Attractive town founded in 1614 by King Christian IV of Denmark. Interesting regional railway museum. ☆ OPEN DAILY EXCEPT MON MAY – SEPT. Film Museum. OPEN TUE, FRI, SUN.

HALLAND

10 Halmstad Museum with fine collection of wall hangings and recently established marine section and extensive model of Halmstad as it was 100 years ago. OPEN DAILY. *Hallansdgården* – an open air museum with 14 preserved buildings. OPEN 24 JUN – 11 AUG. Miniland ☆ (on the outskirts) with models of many of Sweden's most famous buildings. OPEN DAILY IN SUMMER.

11 Ugglarp *Svedinos Bil* and *Flygmuseum*. ☆ An extensive, if somewhat confusing, collection of over 100 vehicles of all kinds and over 30 aircraft from vintage specimens to modern jets. OPEN DAILY IN SUMMER. (Between Tylösand and Falkenberg).

12 Varberg Town with an imposing fortress which also houses a museum (exhibits include the Bocksten Man, the remains of a 14th century man dressed in Middle Ages costume). ☆ MUSEUM OPEN ALL YEAR. Museum of Communications. ☆ Old carriages, boats, cycles and motorcycles. OPEN DAILY 15 JUN – 15 AUG.

13 Tjolöholm Turn of the century house in English Tudor style. Art Nouveau interior. Extensive grounds. OPEN WEEKENDS APR – OCT, TOURS OF THE HOUSE MON – FRI 15 JUN – 15 AUG.

14 Särö Small 19th century seaside resort and now an attractive holiday centre. Excursions by launch in summer to look at seal colonies. ☆

15 Äskhult A collection of four farmhouses in a time warp from the 18th century. (Near Förlanda, S.E. of Kungsbacka).

16 Jätteland (Giant's Land) ☆ A Sommarland with a range of children's attractions. OPEN DAILY IN SUMMER. (At Himle, 3 miles S. of Varberg).

17 Gothenburg Sweden's second largest city and principal port. Laid out by the Dutch with canals and endowed with extensive parks. *Kronhuset* (1643), the oldest secular building, features a history of the city. Numerous other museums include: medical history, military and weapons, natural history, maritime ☆ and art. *Liseberg* ☆ One of Europe's largest and finest amusement parks. OPEN APR – SEPT. 472 acre Botanical Gardens, 342 acre *Slottskogen* with children's zoo ☆ and *Trädgårdsföreningen*, a beautiful park in the city centre. You can tour the canals and harbour in the Paddan boats. *Ramberget*, 282 ft above sea level, provides a splendid panorama of the city and port. Boat excursions to Elfsborg Fortress (1670) on an island in the harbour. Impressive city architecture. See separate chapter on the city.

BOHUSLÄN

18 Uddevalla Bohuslän Museum and Art Museum. Sightseeing boat trips through the archipelago. *Gustafsberg*, on the outskirts, is Sweden's oldest seaside resort.

19 Lysekil Popular seaside resort since the 19th century. Colourful wooden houses in the older part of the town.

20 Tanum The most impressive Bronze Age rock carvings in Sweden are found in this district. Those at *Vitlycke* cover 2,200 sq ft. Others are at *Fossum*, *Tegneby* and *Litsleby*. Large ancient burial ground at *Greby*.

21 Tjörn and Orust Two islands, bridge-connected to the mainland, with delightful rocky coastlines and numerous idyllic little fishing villages.

DALSLAND

22 Håverud The most interesting point on the Dalsland Canal. The canal, built in 1868, is carried over the Upperud river rapids on an aqueduct before entering triple locks. Above are road and rail bridges. Canal museum.

23 Baldersnäs Manor house with Edwardian park, 240 species of trees. Car museum. ☆ OPEN 11 MAY – 1 SEPT.

VÄRMLAND

24 Klässbols Linneväveri Europe's last remaining linen and damask weaving mill using traditional techniques and designs. OPEN WEEKDAYS 8.00 A.M. – 4.00 P.M., SAT 9.00 A.M. – 1.00 P.M.

25 Brunskog Gammelvala (the Old World) 15 old buildings on a picturesque site by Lake Värmeln.

26 Rottneros Impressive manor house on the shores of the Fryken lakes in a 98 acre ornamental park which includes 100 sculptures. OPEN DAILY MAY – END SEPT.

27 Mårbacka Home of Selma Lagerlöf (1858 – 1940), the famous Swedish author who was the first woman to receive a Nobel Prize (for literature, in 1909). Best known for 'The Story of Gösta Berling' and 'The Adventures of Nils Holgersson'. OPEN DAILY MAY 1 – MID SEPT.

28 Tossebergsklätten Mountain, between Sunne and Torsby, providing impressive views over the Fryksdalen valley.

29 Ekshärad 17th century church with baroque interior and grave-yard with wrought iron embellished crosses in place of headstones.

30 Gräsmark 17th century church with ceiling paintings of the Last Judgement. Open air museum which includes Finnish immigrants' cabin and unique photographic archive.

31 Ransäter Well-arranged heritage village with numerous build-ings and four interesting museums documenting the past. ☆ Open air theatre. OPEN DAILY IN SUMMER.

32 Långban *Långban Herrgård* (manor house) was the birthplace of the Ericsson brothers, Nils and John. The former was an eminent railway and canal engineer while the latter invented the screw pro-peller. Restored mining village. This area is rich in minerals of all kinds. (Near Filipstad).

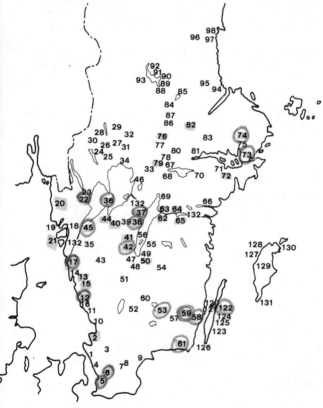

33 Karlskoga *Björkborns Herrgård*. One of Alfred Nobel's houses and now a Nobel museum. GUIDED TOURS DAILY JUNE – AUG.

34 Karlstad Alster Manor (outside the town) – the birthplace (1860) of poet Gustaf Fröding and now a memorial to him. Also a permanent exhibition on the industrial history of Värmland.

VÄSTERGÖTLAND

35 Anten Museum railway with steam trains. ☆ Runs from Anten to *Gräfsnäs* (where there are castle ruins). SUNDAYS 19 MAY – 1 SEPT AND TUESDAYS 11 JUNE – 6 AUG.

✗ **36 Läckö Castle** ☆ One of Sweden's most impressive castles enjoying a superb position on Lake Vänern. Founded in the Middle Ages but the present building is 17th century. In baroque style with 248 rooms. OPEN DAILY IN SUMMER.

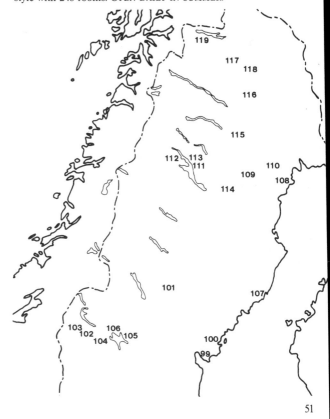

✗ **37 Karlsborg** Huge fortress on the shores of Lake Vättern. ☆ Built between 1819 and 1909 with ramparts 3 miles long. Longest building, the Retrenchment, is 741 yards long. Military museum. GUIDED TOURS EVERY SUN 15 MAY – 15 JUNE and 11 AUG – 14 SEPT and DAILY 16 JUNE – 10 AUG.

✗ **38 Hjo** Charming resort on Lake Vättern with numerous well-preserved wooden houses and pretty lakeside park with an aquarium and butterfly collection. Excursions by the restored 1892 lake steamer 'Trafik'.

39 Skara Sommarland ☆ The biggest of the activity parks with over 70 different things for children, ranging from lunar vehicles to an amazing aqualand. OPEN DAILY 10 MAY – 1 SEPT. (5 miles from Skara).

40 Skara Pleasant town with medieval streets. Cathedral (originally from the 11th century). Skaraborg County Museum. Veterinary Museum. Preserved narrow-gauge railway. ☆

41 Tidaholm Industrial and Motor Museum. ☆ Has examples of the locally-produced motor vehicles built by Tidaholms Bruk (1903 – 1934). A small island in the river has preserved smithies' cottages and the *Turbinshusön* (Turbine House) built in 1898 and now used for art exhibitions.

✗ **42 Habo** Imposing timber church with separate bell tower but with an amazing interior which is entirely covered with paintings which illustrate the Catechism – the work of two men in 1741 – 1743. The organ dates back to 1731.

43 Borås One of Sweden's largest zoos with wild animals in their natural surroundings. ☆ OPEN MAY – SEPT.

44 Lidköping The 'porcelain town' with Sweden's oldest porcelain manufacturer – Rörstrand. OPEN TO VISITORS.

✗ **45 Trollhättan** Imposing Göta Canal locks to overcome the falls. Water is released to rush through the old river bed at 2.00 p.m. Sat & Sun in May and June, and Wed & Sun in July and August.

46 Södra Råda A unique timber church, thought to be 13th century. Interior is completely decorated with naive biblical paintings, the earliest of which are believed to date from 1323. (Near Gullspang).

SMÅLAND

47 Jönköping Busy town on the southern tip of Lake Vättern. Match Museum *(Tändsticksmuseet)* devoted to the history of the match. Includes 9,000 different matchbox labels. OPEN DAILY. Ornithological Museum with 1,400 specimens of stuffed birds. County Museum.

48 Kabe Sommarland ☆ Includes about 40 attractions and activities for children and covers about 359,000 sq yd. OPEN DAILY 16 MAY – 8 SEPT. (Near Jönköping).

49 Huskvarna Dr Skora's *Vaxkabinett* (waxworks). ☆ OPEN DAILY.
Museum of Firearms, Smedbyn. OPEN DAILY, EXCEPT MONDAYS.

50 Riddersberg The studio of one of Sweden's most remarkable
artists, *Calle Örnemark*. ☆ He has produced some fantastic wooden
sculptures including a full-scale interpretation of the Mutiny on the
Bounty and the world's highest wooden statue, the Indian rope
trick, 338 ft high. GROUNDS OPEN TO THE PUBLIC.

51 High Chaparral ☆ The Wild West in Sweden and the dream and
realisation of industrialist Bengt Erlandsson. Complete Wild West
towns with stores, saloon, restaurants, etc. A museum with an
incredible collection of bygones from locomotives to agricultural
implements. Pony and stage coach rides, Wild West steam trains
(with hold-ups!), Indian reservation, animals, daily gun fights in
River City. OPEN DAILY IN SUMMER. (12½ miles from Värnamo).

52 Laganland Car museum with a modest, but beautifully restored,
collection of cars. ☆ OPEN DAILY. (Off the E4).

53 Växjö Småland's Museum. Has a major section on the history
of glass-making. OPEN DAILY. The House of Emigrants. A permanent exhibition covering the 19th century emigration to the USA by
Swedes. OPEN DAILY. Cathedral. Trips on Lake Helga by the 1887
steamer 'Thor'. Kronoberg castle ruins (3 miles N. of Växjö).

54 Eksjö The many old wooden buildings form an attractive
townscape. Museum with exhibits devoted to writer and humorist
Albert Engström. OPEN DAILY. Military museum. Nearby nature
reserve with good views from *Skuruhatt* (1,110 ft above sea level).

55 Gränna Charming small town on the shores of Lake Vättern.
Andrée Museum commemorates S. A. Andrée's unsuccessful at-
tempt to cross the North Pole by balloon in 1897. *Grännaberget*
behind the town offers panoramic views of the lake. The town is
noted for its red and white striped peppermint rock.

56 Visingsö Island in Lake Vättern reached by ferry from *Gränna*
(20 mins). Castle ruins. Interesting baroque church. Superb views
from the old bell tower of Kumlaby Church.

57 Lessebo The Handpapparsbruk still makes paper by hand
using 300-year old methods. GUIDED TOURS ON WEEKDAYS IN
SUMMER.

58 Kalmar A town with a long history and one of the finest castles
in Sweden. Impressive interior with 25 rooms. Also houses the town
museum and a museum devoted to relics of the warship 'Kronan',
sunk in 1676. OPEN DAILY IN SUMMER. Cathedral (1660 - 1703) is the
biggest baroque church in Sweden. Naval Museum. Old walls and
city gates and historic merchants' houses and Empire-style city hall.
Kåremo Aircraft Museum. ☆ OPEN MAY - OCT. (North of Kalmar,
at Ryssby).

59 Kingdom of Glass The region to the west of Kalmar is the heart of the Swedish glass-making industry. Numerous glassworks, many of which are open to visitors including the major ones: *Orrefors*, *Kosta* and *Boda*. Orrefors, for example, is open WEEKDAYS 8.00 A.M. – 3.00 P.M., SATURDAYS 9.00 A.M. – 2.00 P.M., the shop is open daily.

60 Bruk Ohs-Bruk preserved steam railway. ☆ Runs SUNDAYS JUNE – AUG, SATURDAYS IN JULY. (Off road 27, east of Värnamo).

BLEKINGE

61 Karlskrona A naval town founded in 1680. Old shipyard with ropemaking works, Polhems dock and Sweden's first submarine. ☆ GUIDED TOURS DAILY 15 MAY – 31 AUG. A superb Maritime Museum which includes a most impressive collection of ships' figureheads. ☆ OPEN DAILY. Admiralty Church. *Drottningskärs Kastell*, a fort built in 1680. Blekinge Museum, housed in *Grevagården*, a 1705 mansion. OPEN DAILY.

ÖSTERGÖTLAND

62 Vadstena A beautiful little medieval town on Lake Vättern. Renaissance-style 16th century castle. 15th century Abbey. Church of St. Birgitta. Bjälbo Palace dates from 13th century, later became the convent of St. Birgitta, now a museum and hotel. Museum railway. Nearby is Omberg, a hill rising up to 864 ft above sea level and providing wonderful views of Lake Vättern and the surrounding countryside.

63 Motala Göta Canal Museum. ☆ OPEN DAILY 15 MAY – 15 SEPT. Local History Museum in Charlottenborg Castle. Broadcasting and Radio Museum. OPEN DAILY JUNE – AUG. Sightseeing trips on the Göta Canal.

64 Berg Longest flight of locks on the Göta Canal – seven locks in succession raising the water level by 121 ft.

65 Linköping Extensive open air museum *(Gamla Linköping)* gives a good idea of what a Swedish provincial town looked like in the second half of the 19th century. ☆ Over 80 buildings. OPEN DAILY. County Museum. OPEN DAILY. Cathedral – one of Sweden's greatest structural monuments with its 351 ft high spire. Air Force Museum. ☆ OPEN DAILY, EXCEPT SAT. (At Malmslätt).

66 Kolmården Zoo and Safari Park ☆ Covers 400 acres and has 1,000 animals belonging to 100 species. Also terrarium, dolphinarium and waxworks. Aerial cableway, about 2 miles in length. OPEN DAILY 24 MAR – 7 OCT, Safari Park 5 MAY – 23 SEPT.

NÄRKE

67 Örebro Castle with 13th century origins but the present building is 19th century. GUIDED TOURS MID JUNE – MID AUG. Wadköping a selection of preserved buildings in a park. OPEN DAILY IN SUMMER. Huge *Svampen* (mushroom) water tower provides extensive views of the surrounding area, 190 ft above sea level. OPEN DAILY 30 APR – 15 SEPT. County, Technical and Agricultural Museums.

68 Karlslunds Gård A beautifully-proportioned 19th century house surrounded by 90 preserved 18th and 19th century buildings. OPEN DAILY IN SUMMER. (On the outskirts of Örebro).

69 Stjernsund Castle with mid 19th century interior. GUIDED TOURS DAILY MID MAY – END AUG. (South of Askersund).

SÖDERMANLAND

70 Malmköping Vintage tramway museum with over 30 trams. ☆ OPEN WEEKENDS MAY – END SEPT, DAILY IN PEAK SUMMER.

71 Mariefred Veteran steam railway to Läggesta. ☆ WEEKENDS MAY – SEPT, DAILY MIDSUMMER – MID AUG.

72 Gripsholm Castle A majestic 16th century palace in the town of Mariefred. Interior dates from the mid 1500's and houses the State portrait collection. OPEN DAILY MAY – AUG.

73 Stockholm The Swedish capital is dealt with at greater length in a separate chapter and these references merely highlight some of the key attractions. Old Town *(Gamla Stan)* on an island with a fascinating jumble of narrow streets. At one end is the Royal Palace which includes several museums. Djurgården peninsula features *Skansen*, a fine open-air folk museum ☆, the zoo ☆, *Gröna Lund Tivoli* ☆ – a large and lively amusement park – and the Wasa Museum ☆ which houses the 350 year old warship recovered from Stockholm harbour where it sank in 1628. Kaknäs Tower, 508 ft high, offers a bird's eye view of the city. Principal sights include the 17th century Drottningholm Palace (the Royal Family's permanent residence), the Town Hall, Riddarholm Church, 13th century with tombs of many Swedish kings and queens, and the Great Church, 13th century with a splendid baroque interior and wooden sculpture of St. George and the Dragon. There are also some 50 museums to choose from. Also worthwhile are boat trips around the Stockholm area and the archipelago.

UPPLAND

74 Uppsala Site of Sweden's first cathedral and university. The cathedral is the largest church in Scandinavia – 400 ft long, begun in the second half of the 13th century and last restored in 1893 when it received its present spires (almost 400 ft high). Uppsala Castle. OPEN MAR – OCT. Uppland Museum shows the cultural history of the town. OPEN MAY – SEPT. Linnéan Gardens and Museum give an impression of how the great Swedish botanist Carl von Linné lived and worked. Several of the university buildings are impressive,

55

noteworthy being the library, *Carolina Redivivia*, which houses 2 million volumes. Oldest is part of the medical faculty, the *Gustavianum. Gamla Uppsala* has three 6th century royal burial grounds. Museum railway Uppsala-Faringe ☆ OPERATES SUMMER WEEKENDS.

75 Skokloster Mansion with GUIDED TOURS MAY – SEPT. Car Museum ☆ OPEN DAILY.

VÄSTMANLAND

76 Kopparberg Old mining town. Mining Museum, Post Museum, Photographic Museum. 1870 Goldsmith's Workshop. Old Homestead Museum with costumes and bygones.

77 Stjernfors Manor House with adjoining museums devoted to minerals, old cars, telecommunications and curiosities. ☆ OPEN WED – SUN IN SUMMER, WEEKENDS IN MAY AND AUG.

78 Nora Former centre of the iron industry. Old buildings. Museum. Veteran Railway. ☆

79 Pershyttan Well preserved smelting house and waterwheel. (S. of Nora).

80 Bergslagen This area was the centre of the mining industry in the 18th and 19th centuries. Numerous preserved smelting houses and other artefacts. *Siggebohyttan* has a master miner's homestead. OPEN DAILY IN SUMMER. (Between Nora and Lindesberg). *Löa Hytta* has a preserved smelting house with explanatory details. CONDUCTED TOURS IN SUMMER. (Between Lindesberg and Kopparberg). *Stråssa Gruva* is a mine in which you can ride a mine train 60 ft underground. ☆ OPEN DAILY IN SUMMER. (N.E. of Stora).

81 Surahammar Foundry museum with implements and models.

82 Norberg *Polhemshjulet* – a 49 ft diameter water wheel constructed by Christopher Polhem.

83 Sala Silver Mine – Queen Christine's Pit – which you can go down. ☆ OPEN IN SUMMER.

DALARNA

84 Borlänge *Gammelgården* – a collection of 31 old buildings in which there are 30,000 relics. One building is a museum dedicated to opera singer Jussi Björling. OPEN DAILY. Geological Museum. OPEN DAILY. Motor Museum with old cars, motorcycles and old toys. ☆ OPEN AT WEEKENDS II MAY – 20 JUNE and I2 AUG – I SEPT, DAILY 2I JUNE – II AUG. (At Torsång, 5 miles from Borlänge).

85 Falun The 'Copper Town'. You can descend 197 ft into the mine. Guided tours in summer. Stora Kopparberg Museum. Collections of a technical and industrial nature. Dalarna's Museum includes local costumes and peasant paintings.

86 Grängesberg Railway museum which includes the world's only remaining steam turbine locomotive in working order. ☆

87 Ludvika *Ludvika Gammelgård* is a particularly good mining museum with reconstructed mine, winding house, underground railway and miners' houses. ☆

88 Leksand Open air museum with an extensive collection of buildings. OPEN IN SUMMER. Boat trips on the lake.

89 Hjortnäs Tin figures museum with dioramas depicting historical scenes. ☆ OPEN DAILY IN SUMMER.

90 Rättvik Gammelgård A collection of old buildings with period contents. OPEN IN SUMMER. Natural History Museum. Lakeside church, oldest part from the 14th century.

91 Nusnäs Workshops where they produce and sell the traditional hand-painted Dalecarlian horses. ☆ OPEN IN SUMMER. (6 miles S. of Mora on the eastern shore of Lake Siljan).

92 Mora Beautifully situated town on Lake Siljan. Church, part of which dates from 1200, has a 1672 bell tower. One of Sweden's best known artists Anders Zorn (1860 - 1920) lived here. His home is open to visitors. The Zorn Museum has a large collection of his paintings. Island of Sollerön (reached by a bridge) has over 100 Viking graves. Boat trips on the lake including excursions by the 1876 steamship Gustaf Wasa. Forestry Museum (Skogsmuseum). OPEN DAILY IN SUMMER. (Outside the town on road 242).

93 Gesunda Mountain 1,690 ft above sea level. Part way up is *Tomteland* (Santaworld). ☆ The 'home' of Santa Claus and his friends and helpers. Attractions include Santa's Workshop, Snow Queen's Palace, Sleigh House, etc. OPEN IN SUMMER. (Near Mora).

GÄSTRIKLAND

94 Gävle Old Gefle – a collection of old wooden houses. County Museum with about 16,000 objects. OPEN DAILY. Forestry Museum. Castle. Railway Museum. ☆ Has 29 locomotives, 27 vehicles, many models and small exhibits. OPEN DAILY.

95 Jädraås Museum railway with steam trains to Tallås. ☆ OPERATES SUN, END MAY – MID SEPT.

HÄLSINGLAND

96 Järvsö Attractive little resort in the Ljusnan valley. Church – on an island in the river – is the largest country church in Sweden. *Stenegård* – a well-preserved manor house with a number of workshops where craftsmen (blacksmith, silversmith, glass blower, potter, etc.) can be seen at work.

97 Boda Caves Largest caves in Sweden and the longest system of primary rock caves in Europe. GUIDES AVAILABLE SAT, JUNE – SEPT.

98 Hudiksvall Fishermen's old houses and old wooden wharves and warehouses. Hälsingland Museum.

ÅNGERMANLAND

99 Härnösand Regional open air and historical museum, nicely sited on a hilltop. Includes about 80 buildings. OPEN IN SUMMER. Interesting buildings in the old town (Östanbäcken). Cathedral – 19th century. Beautiful town hall (1791) in classic style.

100 Höga Kusten The High Coast, a very beautiful coastal area between *Örnsköldsvik* and *Härnösand*. Near Dockstra is the *Skuleberget* (964 ft above sea level) which is an interesting nature area.

101 Hoting Car Museum with about 50 vehicles. ☆ OPEN DAILY JUNE – AUG.

JÄMTLAND

102 Åre Principally a winter sports resort. Well preserved church (13th century). Åreskutan Mountain (4,658 ft above sea level). Cable car to 4,179 ft. The summit can be ascended without undue difficulty and offers splendid views.

103 Tännforsen Impressive waterfall with a vertical fall of 105 ft. (W. of Åre).

104 Ristafallet Another waterfall with a fall of 46 ft. (Near Hålland, E. of Åre).

105 Östersund Pleasant town on the shore of Lake Storsjön. Jamtli is one of the largest and finest open air museums in Sweden. ☆ In summer you can see 18th and 19th century life in action: baking, spinning, farming, etc. Covers nearly a square mile in area. OPEN DAILY. County Museum – has 40,000 items. OPEN DAILY. The 1875 steamer 'Thomée' provides excursions on the lake. SAILS JUNE – MID AUG.

106 Frösön Island, bridge-connected to Östersund. Frösö church dates from 13th century and has a separate 18th century bell tower. Frösö tower is the island's highest point (1,578 ft above sea level). Lift to an enclosed viewing platform. OPEN DAILY. Home of noted Swedish composer and music critic Wilhelm Peterson-Berger (1867 – 1942). OPEN DAILY 8 MAY – 18 AUG.

VÄSTERBOTTEN

107 Umeå Preserved old buildings in the Gammlia park where there is also the County Museum.

NORRBOTTEN

108 Luleå The original town – now called the old town *(Gammelstad)* – is about 6 miles inland from the present centre of *Luleå*. The Old Town is dominated by the church dating back to the Middle Ages. Around it is the fascinating church town consisting of about 500 buildings. Even the more recent houses are of the same type as the older ones and occupy the original sites. In modern Luleå is the Norrbottens Museum which is devoted to the region's history and culture.

109 Storfossen Impressive falls which extend over 3 miles, during which the river drops 269 ft. (Near Älvsbyn).

110 Boden Largest garrison town in Sweden. *Garnisonsmuseet*, the Garrison Museum, shows the development of the armed forces over the last 400 years. ☆

SOUTHERN LAPLAND

111 Arjeplog Beautifully situated small town on the islets between Lakes Hornavan and Uddjaure. On the 'Silver Road' which links the Gulf of Bothnia and the Norwegian port of Bodø. The Silver Museum ☆ has a superb collection of Lappish silver and also many other items relating to the Lapps and their life and history. The museum was created by the 'Doctor of the Lapps', Einer Wallqvist.

112 Laisvall One of the biggest lead mines in Europe which is run by a modern but isolated community in the middle of the wilderness. OPEN MON – FRI, MIDSUMMER – AUG (no children under 15 years of age).

113 Galtisbuouda Mountain (2,624 ft above sea level) about 6 miles from Arjeplog and providing impressive views in all directions. Road to the summit.

114 Arvidsjaur Has a Lapp village with about 80 examples of the two different types of Lapp houses – the *Kåtor* and *Härbren*.

115 Jokkmokk On the Arctic Circle. Museum devoted to local history and the Lapps.

NORTHERN LAPLAND

116 Gällivare One of two major centres for the mining of iron ore. Museum at Malmberget shows the development of mining in the area. Dundret Mountain (2,690 ft above sea level) offers magnificent views. (About 6 miles from Gällivare).

117 Kiruna Largest town in northern Sweden; dominated by the world's largest iron ore mine. Tours of the mine run daily. Tramway Museum. ☆ OPERATES SUN 1 JUNE – 25 AUG, WED/THUR 5 JUNE – 27 JULY.

118 Jukkasjärvi Folk Museum with old buildings. Centre for exciting trips through the rapids on a rubber raft.

119 Nordkalottvägen The new highway linking Kiruna and Narvik (Norway), the final section of which was opened in 1984. Winds 105 miles through some of the finest scenery in Scandinavia. Particularly beautiful alongside Lake Torne Träsk.

ÖLAND

120 Borgholm Imposing castle ruins.

121 Solliden Royal summer residence built 1903/6. Park open to the public JUNE – AUG.

✗ **122 Störlinge** Longest row of windmills (seven) on the island. Altogether there are 400 windmills.

123 Eketorps Borg Remains of 5th century fortress now reconstructed to show how life was lived 1,500 years ago. OPEN DAILY MAY – SEPT.

124 Gärdslösa Best preserved of the island's medieval churches.

125 Gråborg Ancient fortress and ruins of St. Knut's Chapel (13th century).

126 Ottenby Bird sanctuary and ornithological museum. OPEN IN SUMMER.

GOTLAND

127 Visby Former Hanseatic town. The wall stretching almost 2 miles around the town is one of Europe's biggest and best preserved structures from the Middle Ages. Town has many half-timbered houses.

128 Lummelundagrottorna Large limestone caves. ☆ OPEN DAILY IN SUMMER.

129 Romakloster Ruins of a 12th century monastery.

130 Bunge Open air museum with preserved buildings, etc. OPEN IN SUMMER.

131 Hoburgen Fascinating limestone stacks on the coast.

GÖTA CANAL

132 Göta Canal This waterway, built 1810–32, stretches from the Göta river at Gothenburg all the way to Stockholm on the Baltic – a distance of 322 miles. About one third consists of artificial canals while the remainder makes use of rivers and lakes. Most impressive features are the 65 locks which raise vessels to a height of over 300 ft above sea level and then bring them down to sea level again. It is worth seeing one of the flights of locks and those at *Trollhättan*, *Berg* and *Borenshult* are recommended. You can take short excursions on the canal from various points or sail on one of the renowned Göta Canal steamers the entire distance (3 days).

NOTE: *General literature issued by the Swedish Tourist Board and brochures published by the various regional and local tourist offices provide additional information on places of interest and current times of opening.*

SHOPPING

DESIGN AND QUALITY are the two most notable features of the majority of Swedish merchandise and this combination offers the visitor a justifiable excuse to run amok in individual shops and department stores.

There is a wide range of attractive products, but heading the list must be Swedish glass followed by stainless steel, silver, pottery and ceramics, textiles, jewellery, leather goods and articles made from wood.

If you are within striking distance of the 'glass country', that area of south east Sweden west of Kalmar, then visit the glassworks of *Orrefors*, *Boda* or *Kosta*. All of them – and many of the smaller companies as well – have shops attached to their factories where you can buy 'seconds' at greatly reduced prices.

You can also buy fine porcelain in Sweden and you can discover bargains at the *Gustavsberg* factory outside Stockholm and at the old-established *Rörstrand* factory at Lidköping.

The area centred on *Borås* is the weaver's country where the textile firms are based and where you will come across some good buys at the factory shops and bargain stores. 'Knallebygden' is a large shopping centre in Borås where attractive low-cost clothing is sold by leading direct mail companies. Modern fashionable clothing at reasonable prices can be found at *Hennes & Mauritz* (H & M) which has branches all over Sweden.

If you are interested in furs (rather more expensive souvenirs) then the centre of this business is *Tranås* in the county of Småland. Here again, you can come across some relative bargains and perhaps this is a suitable point to mention that all the well-known credit cards are widely accepted in Sweden, as are Eurocheques and travellers' cheques.

For elegant furniture and fittings for the home, look around one of the *IKEA* stores which are usually to be found on the outskirts of towns. I haven't been to one recently but I know they have a well-founded reputation for low prices. These stores are often open on Sundays and, more importantly, they operate an export service.

There are several well-known Swedish department stores including *NK* (which calls itself Scandinavia's largest store), *Åhlens* and its associated stores called *Domus* and *Pub* (only in Stockholm). You will also find shopping centres and shopping 'warehouses' often on the edge of cities and towns, one with numerous branches being *Obs!*

Many towns have pedestrain precincts which making browsing an enjoyable occupation while there are also shopping malls, like *Gallerian* in Stockholm and *Nordstan* in Gothenburg.

Many exciting designs can be found in smaller shops and boutiques which flourish in major cities and towns. Also you shouldn't overlook the wide range of Swedish handicrafts – such as items made from birch bark (a Lapp speciality), pewter, handwoven textiles, embroidery, ceramics and, of course, the famous brightly-painted Dala horses. You can see these being made and buy them at the factory shop at *Nusnäs*, near Mora on Lake Siljan. Further north you will find the Lapp handicrafts and reindeer skins.

In the country, while driving along, you will come across small workshops and studios where artists and craftsmen create a variety of things from pottery to paintings which can often be bought at very reasonable prices. The handicraft centres *(Hemslöjd)* are another source of attractively produced items: clothes, glass, jewellery, metalwork, wooden objects to mention just some of them.

OPENING TIMES

Most shops open between 9.00 a.m. – 6.00 p.m. on weekdays and close on Saturdays in the afternoon (can be any time between 1.00 p.m. – 4.00 p.m.) while there is late night shopping one evening a week. In some larger towns the department stores remain open until 8.00 p.m. or even 10.00 p.m. while some also open on Sundays. For example NK in Stockholm is open 9.30 a.m. to 7.00 p.m., Mondays to Fridays, 9.30 a.m. to 5.00 p.m. on Saturdays and 11.00 a.m. to 4.00 p.m. on Sundays. Åhlens in Stockholm have their ground floor open later than the normal 9.30 a.m. – 6.00 p.m., while the basement and food department is open from 9.30 a.m. – 9.00 p.m. Mondays to Saturdays and 11.00 a.m. – 9.00 p.m. on Sundays.

In the country, shops usually close at 5.00 p.m. to 6.00 p.m. although in holiday areas some food shops will be open on Sundays.

Two points worth noting: summer is when most Swedish stores hold their sales – look for stickers with the word 'Rea' on the windows. Also, shops generally close early the day before a public holiday.

SHOPPING FOR FOOD

If you are self-catering or want to have picnics the easiest solution is the local supermarket. There are various chains, such as *ICA* which is a voluntary chain of about 4,000 privately-owned stores. They fall into four categories: supermarkets with a large range of fresh food and specialities; local shops with fresh food and some specialities; city centre stores which stock a smaller range of fresh foods; and country stores *(Lanthandel)* which offer some fresh food and specialities. Another one is *Konsum* (food and dairy products).

As English is so widely spoken you should be able to find someone – staff or customer – who can help you out if you are mystified by the contents of a package or cannot find the product you are looking for.

Should you be indulging in picnics – and there are certainly plenty of opportunities for them in Sweden – then don't forget to take some knives and forks (plastic ones will do) while a cold bag is very useful. There are plenty of lay-bys and pleasant areas for picnics; quite a few have toilets and they nearly always have litter bins or sacks. Please use the latter, not only to keep Sweden tidy but to avoid wild animals ingesting something which might be harmful to them.

Another thing to remember is that you can only buy alcoholic drinks (except beer of classes I and II) at the state monopoly *Systembolaget* shops. These are open from 9.00 a.m. – 6.00 p.m. Mondays to Fridays only, being closed at weekends.

TAX-FREE SHOPPING

Value added tax *(Moms)* is currently 19 per cent and as a visitor living outside the Nordic area you can recover the VAT you have paid on goods you have purchased. There are roughly 8,500 shops in this tax-free scheme and they are identified by the Tax Free for Tourists sticker they display. The VAT is repaid in cash when you leave Sweden – at harbours, ferry terminals, airports and on board certain ships.

You show your passport when you make a purchase and the shop assistant will write out a Tax Free Shopping Check and you complete the reverse of this document. The goods you buy must not be used in Sweden and they have to be taken out of the country within seven days of purchase.

When you leave Sweden you show the article you have purchased and the tax free document at the repayment office and then the VAT amount is given to you.

You can go through this procedure for a refund on board the DFDS Seaways ships on the Harwich route and also on the ferries operated by various lines between Sweden and Denmark and at the land frontiers with Norway and Finland.

A tax-free guide is available which gives full details of the scheme and also lists those shops participating as well as providing details of the offices where you can recover the VAT.

SPORTS AND RECREATIONS

THE SWEDES CARE passionately about sports and physical recreation and, for example, nearly a quarter of the population belongs to one or other of the 56 specialised national associations within the Swedish Sports Federation. Facilities for sports and outdoor activities are very good and most of them are available to visitors. Everything is well organised and if you haven't got the right equipment you can nearly always hire it.

Swimming and bathing With Sweden's long coastline and vast number of lakes there are endless opportunities for swimming and bathing. The west coast provides the best bathing beaches – particularly in the county of *Halland*. Beyond Gothenburg the coastline is rocky but equally good for bathing. The east coast also has its quota of beaches from *Piteå* in the north, right down to the southernmost tip of the country. The island of *Öland* has some pleasant beaches while there are good bathing beaches on the island of *Gotland*. Both islands can be crowded in the short peak summer season but are largely deserted at other times.

All beaches are open freely to the public and are not really 'developed' as they are in some countries. Nude bathing is permitted on some beaches and topless bathing and sunbathing is commonplace.

There are plenty of lakes where you can swim, but some of these can be cold and others are very deep. Recommended lakeside or seaside beaches are always signposted.

Fishing It is claimed that one out of every three Swedes is an angler and with such an abundance of well-stocked rivers and lakes the popularity of the sport is understandable. If you wish to fish in any lakes, rivers or streams you need a licence apart from Lakes *Vänern*, *Vättern*, *Mäleren*, *Hjälmaren* and *Storsjön*. The cost of a licence varies from one area to another, but you will be able to get full information from the local tourist office. In spite of the popularity of angling there are plenty of places where you can fish undisturbed.

The *Domänverket* organisation (Sweden's National Board of Crown Lands and Forests) controls the fishing rights in 6,000 lakes as well as hundreds of miles of river. Their subsidiary, *Sverek*, manages tourist sites and handles reservations for chalet rental. Brochure obtainable from Sverek/Domän Turist, S-171 93 Solna.

In southern and central Sweden you will find pike, pike-perch, perch and eel while further north trout and grayling are abundant, also arctic char which is the most characteristic cold water fish. The *Mörrumsån* river in the county of Blekinge is renowned for its salmon. There are excellent opportunities for coarse fishing.

Sea fishing from a boat, or off the shore, is unrestricted and there are good opportunities along the west coast. In *Skåne*, *Halland* and *Bohuslän* counties sea fishing trips are run during the summer.

A leaflet on angling in Sweden is available from the Swedish National Tourist Office in London. One last point: you can fish for salmon and trout in the waters around the centre of Stockholm, and you don't even need a licence. You can get a leaflet about it from the Stockholm Information Service.

Canoeing and Sailing Canoeing is a tremendously popular pastime and you can hire canoes, either by the day or the week, all over the country. A day's hire will be around Skr50. There are also numerous packages, the price of which will cover the canoe and equipment. The latter will really be all-embracing, right down to a bag to put your garbage in. Where other items may be required these are invariably available on hire. Hotels, self-catering villages or camping sites by lakes frequently have canoes and boats for hire. You can also hire motor boats, sailing boats and motor cruisers.

Rafting This can take two forms, either white water rafting or river rafting. The former means an exhilarating journey along a fast-moving river, punctuated by a series of rapids, in an inflatable rubber boat. There are day trips and week-long excursions in Lapland using the *Torne*, *Kalix* and *Kaitum* rivers. A skilled leader accompanies each boat (details from Jukkasjärvi, Box 24, S-980 21 Jukkasjärvi).

River rafting, by contrast, is very tranquil. You can hire a pontoon raft or build your own log raft and drift gently down the slow moving *Klarälven* river in Värmland – a process which takes about a week. When you build your own raft you are provided with logs, ropes and instructions and your raft building is supervised. You sleep in a tent and cook your own food and at journey's end you take your raft apart and the logs continue on their way to eventually end up at a timber yard or paper mill. Full details from Vildmark i Värmland AB, Sundbergsvägen 13, S-685 00 Torsby.

Golf Sweden claims to be the most golf-conscious country in Europe after Britain. There are 187 courses which are rarely crowded and town courses in summer are often deserted. Visitors are welcome but you should take your local membership card or a letter from your club secretary. Green fees vary, but average between Skr40 and Skr130.

If you are going to Lapland you can even play by the light of the midnight sun on the most northerly course in Europe.

Further information on Swedish clubs and courses can be had from Svenska Golfförbundet, Kevinge, S-182 31 Danderyd. The Swedish National Tourist Office in London also has available a brochure on golf in Sweden.

Riding There are many riding schools and riding stables throughout Sweden and prices are reasonable by UK standards. For those who already have some riding ability there are riding tours of varying duration and, for example, you can try a one week pony trek in the region of *Knebnekaise*, Sweden's highest mountain.

Walking With hundreds of miles of marked trails there are endless opportunities for walking. But you don't have to become a backpacker and disappear for days, there are plenty of quite gentle hikes taking only a few hours. There are also guided walks and information on these and the trails in the surrounding area will be available from any local tourist office.

Cycling A large part of Sweden is excellent cycling country and there are plenty of places where you can hire a bicycle by the day or for a longer period. Typical hire cost: Skr30 a day or Skr150 a week. There are many miles of special cycle tracks and details of these, plus general information on cycling in Sweden, is available from the Swedish Cycling Association, Box 6006, S-163 06 Spånga.

Other activities Jogging, along marked tracks; tennis, many very good courts, particularly in the south (remember this is Bjorn Borg country); windsurfing and water ski-ing; climbing, including glacier climbing in the north; gliding; bird watching, popular in southern and central Sweden (more details from the Swedish Touring Club, Box 25, S-101 20 Stockholm); panning for gold (no guarantee you will find any); and even summer ski-ing on the slopes of *Kebnetjåkkos*.

To give some idea of the range of activities available I have picked out two places, which are in no way exceptional: *Kopparberg* – canoeing, fishing, cross-country riding, golf, tennis, elk safari, looking for minerals, panning for gold, stone polishing, basket painting and basketry; Dundret Holiday Centre, *Gällivare* – windsurfing, golf, fishing, walking, riding, canoeing, shooting the rapids and panning for gold.

Right of Public Access In Sweden everyone has freedom of access to the countryside and this is covered by the Right of Public Access or, as it is sometimes called, everyman's right. It allows you to walk freely in woods, fields and meadows, and to pick wild mushrooms, berries and flowers (except those that are protected) and to go swimming or boating on lakes or watercourses.

You can walk, jog, cycle or ride across people's land providing you do not damage crops or forest plantations but you are not entitled to cross or stay on private plots without permission. You can pitch a tent for a day or two on land which is not being used for farming or which is not close to a dwelling house. You are not allowed to take your car or motor cycle off the road or on roads closed to motor traffic or private roads *(Enskild väg)*.

There are also conditions relating to where you may swim or tie up a boat, light a fire and so on. This freedom does, quite rightly, impose obligations so that the natural environment and wildlife is not disturbed. A useful booklet which explains the Right of Public Access has been published by the National Environmental Protection Board and is available from the Swedish National Tourist Office in London.

THE ITINERARIES – AN INTRODUCTION

WITH A COUNTRY the size of Sweden it is obvious that the itineraries in this book represent only a few of the possibilities that are available to the motorist. I have concentrated on the more interesting areas, but have also borne in mind that most of us have a limit on the amount of time (and money) that we can spend on a holiday.

The duration of each itinerary has been kept within reasonable bounds, although in most instances there are options for extending your stay. I have also suggested additional excursions where these are appropriate – for example, to Stockholm which is not included directly in any of the itineraries. I would certainly recommend including a visit to the Swedish capital which has many places of interest and enjoys a wonderful location.

All the routes in the itineraries have been personally checked within the last year, with one or two exceptions. In some examples I give alternative routes which depend on whether you like minor roads or prefer to keep to main highways. You can of course do a lot of additional exploring by extending your overnight stops, but do make sure you have a good map with you.

In the earlier chapter on 'Driving in Sweden' I have recommended the road maps published by Esselte. There are eight of them covering the entire country. At the end of the introduction to each itinerary I have indicated which maps you will require for that particular journey.

I have laid particular stress on road numbers in guiding you on your way, as these are easier to follow in many instances than place names. There are the international 'E' roads while national highways are numbered between 1 and 99. County roads are numbered from 100 upwards.

In the chapter 'Attractions for Children and Adults' the various entries are numbered and where these are also referred to in the itineraries they are cross-referenced with the same number. You should refer to these entries as this information is not necessarily repeated in the itineraries. Also, any attractions of special interest to children are indicated with a ☆.

Where I have visited hotels and restaurants they are described in more detail. Those that are merely listed may be perfectly satisfactory, but it is simply a case of having no personal knowledge of them. Camping sites and youth hostels are only mentioned from time to time – to include a reference to all of them would have required a greatly expanded book. But Sweden is well endowed with a great many camping sites and has some delightfully located youth hostels.

I would also like to stress that the Swedish summer season is short (I am not referring to the climate in this instance) and that many places of interest are only open for a limited period. This is something which I hope the Swedish tourist authorities will try and use their influence to have changed. Early summer and autumn are enjoyable times in which to make your visit, even if you have to restrict your cultural intake because some of the museums and other attractions are closed.

Mileages have not, in general, been included as there are so many possible variations that it would be very difficult to give accurate figures. In every case the daily distances are not demanding, given the modest amount of traffic you will encounter on Swedish roads.

DEFENCE AREAS

A part of northern Sweden, some of the Swedish coastline and the north-eastern tip of Gotland and the adjoining island of Fårö are all designated defence areas. There are restrictions on foreigners visiting these areas and some confusion exists on the law on this point. According to the Swedish Ministry of Defence aliens may, without permission, remain within a restricted area for a maximum of 72 hours including the time taken to reach and leave the stopping place.

The regulations go on to say that: 'Journeys within restricted areas will be made without unnecessary stops and shall be for the purpose of direct passage through the area or movement to or from places which aliens are permitted to visit'. There are multi-lingual notices on roads which enter these defence areas.

The unusual aqueduct on the Dalsland Canal at Haverud.

Many towns have pedestrianised their principal shopping streets and typical is Kungsgatan in Gothenburg, Sweden's second largest city.

ABOVE – The landscape of the island of Öland is notable for the number of preserved wooden windmills.

BELOW – There are numerous small picturesque fishing villages along the west coast. This placid scene is at Grundsund.

Narrow little streets abound in the historic walled town of Visby on the island of Gotland.

ABOVE – Not to be missed on a visit to Stockholm is the fascinating Gamla Stan or Old Town.

BELOW – The attractive Kungsträdgården in the heart of Stockholm. In the background is Hamngatan, one of the principal shopping streets.

A feature of old Swedish churches is the separate wooden bell tower.
This very fine example is on the island of Frösö, near Östersund.

ABOVE – With the extensive coastline there is no shortage of safe bathing beaches.

BELOW – In many towns the old wooden buildings are now subject to preservation. Some charming examples are to be found at Eksjö.

The far north offers scenery on a grand scale. In this photograph the country's highest mountain, Kebnekaise, can be seen in the background.

ALONG THE WEST COAST

THIS ITINERARY takes you first across Denmark and then over the Sound to Sweden providing the opportunity of spending a night in Copenhagen. Your journey will take you along Sweden's enchanting west coast beginning in one corner of the county of Skåne, which has certain similarities to Denmark. You can visit the popular resort of Båstad, where there are good beaches, and then move on either to Halmstad or Tylösand for an overnight stay.

You potter along the coast, avoiding the main E6 road wherever possible and call at Falkenberg and Varberg with its massive fortress. Another diversion is to the remarkable Tudor-style castle at Tjolöholm after which you make for the charming coastal village of Särö, your next overnight stop.

After skirting Gothenberg, Sweden's second largest city, your exploration of the west coast leads you on to the islands of Tjörn and Orust with their picturesque little fishing villages which cling to the rocky coastline. You have the alternative of staying at the resort of Lysekil or the town of Uddevalla. The next section of this coastal journey is particularly beautiful and continues to Grebbestad where you move inland to Tanumshede. In the immediate vicinity is an amazing collection of Bronze Age rock carvings.

At this point you can make an excursion into Norway or even to the capital, Oslo, or you can spend some time on the coast. A further day's motoring lets you enjoy some of the scenic pleasures of Dalsland county and to visit the intriguing aqueduct on the Dalsland canal at Håverud (illustrated on page 69). You return by a different route to Gothenburg for your final night in Sweden and it is from here that you sail back to Britain.

You can complete this itinerary with seven nights in Sweden, but it would be preferable to extend your stay to nine or ten nights, spending more time on the coast. *Maps 1 and 2.*

DAY 1

Leave Esbjerg on the E66, drive across Jutland and the island of Funen and then take the ferry over the Great Belt to Zealand (crossing time 50 minutes, reservation recommended). The E66 merges with the E4 and after that you should follow the E4 signs to Helsingør. This skirts Copenhagen and where the motorway ends, near Helsingør, it is clearly signed to the ferry for the 25 minute crossing to Helsingborg (1). There are two ferry operators at Helsingør – DSB/SJ and Scandinavian Ferry Lines; they go from different berths and both have very frequent sailings, up to 50 a day.

Leave Helsingborg on road 22 which follows the coast via Höganäs to *Mölle*, an attractive little harbour town on the southern slopes of Kullaberg. The Grand Hotel, in an elevated position, provides beautiful views across the Kattegat and Öresund to Denmark and makes a comfortable overnight stay. There is also Kullagårdens Wärdshus. Alternatively you can turn right before reaching Mölle and after about four miles turn left to *Arild*, a very pretty village which descends quite steeply to a tiny harbour. On the left as you come into the village is the Rusthållargården, a splendid old-established hotel (see Country Living for a description of it). Also at Arild is the Strand Hotel.

DAY 2

The immediate district around Mölle and Arild is charming with its local 'mountain' the Kullaberg (620ft above sea level) and with cliffs descending to the sea. If you are extending the basic itinerary you could well spend an extra night in this area. Otherwise you leave Mölle/Arild on the secondary road which joins the 112 at Jonstorp and then on reaching the E6 turn left. An alternative is to follow signs to Angelholm and then take the secondary road via Grevie and Torekov (a popular seaside village) to *Båstad* (**2**). This resort is closely associated with tennis and the Swedish Open Championships are held here. You can also play golf (two courses), bathe (sandy beaches) or go fishing. Beyond Båstad are further beaches at Skummeslövsstrand and Mellbystrand.

On the E6 you follow the signs to *Halmstad* (**10**), going through the commercial district before reaching the heart of the town by the river. Noticeable is the sail training ship 'Najaden', while attractions include some old 17th century houses, the castle and Halmstad Museum which has a fine collection of wall hangings, a new marine section, plus a large model of the town as it was in the past. On the outskirts is Miniland, which includes models of well known buildings in Sweden.

The Grand Hotel (near the station, street parking) is an excellent place to stay. Built in 1907, it has recently been extensively redecorated and refurnished and now has very comfortable rooms. There is a first class restaurant – the Grand Gourmet – while the breakfast buffet provides an impressive choice. The reception is friendly and welcoming. Other hotels include the Continental, Hallandia (Scandic) and the Mårtensson. The alternative place to stay is on the coast at Tylösand.

DAY 3

Drive to Tylösand, only a few miles from Halmstad, which is called the Swedish Riviera and very much a holiday centre. It reminded me a little of the area around Le Touquet. There are some long stretches of sandy beach with good bathing. Dominating Tylösand is the recently expanded and renovated Nya Tylösand Hotel which has 230 bedrooms, a vast restaurant, a big indoor pool, sauna, solarium, bar, disco and tennis courts. It now sprawls over a considerable area which means that you can have a long walk, for example, to the restaurant. It adjoins the sandhills and beach. There are two golf courses in the immediate area.

Leave Tylösand on the secondary coast road to Falkenberg via Gullbrandstorp and Haverdal. Just beyond Stensjö you will see on

the right Svedinos Bil och Flygmuseum (**11**) ☆ which has 140 old
cars and some 31 old and new aircraft on display. Something of an
Aladdin's Cave for those interested in vintage aircraft and motor
vehicles. There are some unusual items like the 1897 Bullerbilen
car, and more familiar ones like the De Havilland 60 biplane.

Join the E6 and then leave it again if you want to go into
Falkenberg. There are no great attractions here but it does have
some colourful old wooden houses around the 14th century church.
Rejoin the E6 and leave it to enter *Varberg* (**12**) which is a fair sized
town with a ferry connection to Denmark. Beside the harbour in a
little park is the delightful 1883 societetshuset (pavilion), which is
now a restaurant. Nearby is the massive Varberg fortress which is
well worth seeing, while the Varberg Museum in the same building
includes the Bocksten Man – the remains of a 14th century man
dressed in the only completely preserved Middle Ages costume. In
the fortress stables is the Museum of Communication. There is a
gently shelving beach, suitable for children, not far away at
Apelviken.

You could make this your overnight stop if you wished or add it
to the basic itinerary. Varberg has a number of hotels, the biggest
being the Hotel Statt (126 rooms, part of the Sara chain).

About six miles short of Varberg on the E6 there is a right turn
to Himle where you will find Jätteland (Giant's Land) – one of the
Sommarland activity parks for children (**16**) ☆.

Continue on the E6 and leave it where it is signed to Värö – you
go under the main road and then turn right just short of the rail-

79

way. This is a secondary road which parallels the railway (on the left) and the E6 (on the right). Beyond Åsa look for the road on the left to Tjolöholm and this will take you to Tjolöholm Castle (**13**) which was built at the turn of the century in 16th century Tudor style. It looks as though it has been moved lock, stock and barrel from somewhere in England and has an impressive art nouveau interior (which you can see).

Rejoin the road from Åsa and follow signs to Kungsbacka, ignoring the E6. In the town centre follow the signs to *Särö* (road 158). You go past the golf course and then the tennis courts and finally come down to the sea. Perched above the shore you will see the Säröhus Hotel which enjoys a splendid position overlooking the rocky coastline. For a description of this comfortable hotel see the Country Living itinerary.

Särö (**14**) became a popular seaside resort in the middle of the 19th century and regular visitors included members of the Swedish royal family. It still has a turn of the century atmosphere. You can go and see the seal colony, hire a boat or go walking in the oldest oak woods on the west coast. By the sea is the Särö Värdshus, a restaurant housed in the old railway station.

DAY 4

Return to Kungsbacka, which has a rather pleasant market place surrounded by attractive wooden buildings, and rejoin the E6. Follow the E6 Oslo signs through Gothenburg, bypass Küngälv and at Jörlanda, roughly 20 miles from Gothenburg, take a left turn on road 160 to Orust and Tjörn (**21**). This road parallels the E6 and the coast, and just short of Stenungsund you bear left, go over a bridge and through a short tunnel and then over a second and very impressive bridge. Then, when you come to a set of traffic lights, turn left (marked to Rönnäng).

Ignore Rönnäng and go to *Klädesholmen* which is on a tiny island, linked by a modern bridge, and is tightly packed with a colourful jumble of wooden houses. They look as though they are clinging to the rocky surface, as indeed they are. There is a car park just before the bridge which gives you a good view of the village, and the skerries which are such a feature of this coastline. Here and there the view is spoiled by industrial buildings – usually connected with fish processing.

Further along the coast is *Skärhamn* which also has narrow streets, little wooden houses and a small square in the centre. Continue through Kållekär and turn left on to road 160 (signed to Orust). After passing through pleasant scenery you reach Orust over a magnificent curved bridge which provides lovely views in both directions. Just beyond the bridge is a parking and picnic place on the left.

At the next crossroads turn left to Mollösund on a small road which climbs quite steeply through scenery which is a mix of rocks, water and small inlets. Instead of going to Mollösund, you turn towards Hälleviksstrand and later turn left to Ellös. Here you can take the small ferry (crossing time 10 minutes) to Rågardsvik and continue to *Grundsund*, which requires a left turn. This is another attractive little fishing village with tightly packed wooden houses and fishermen's huts. If you drive through the village, over a bridge and past the church, you can then drop down to the quayside. 'Picturesque' is an overworked word but it is justified when used to describe Grundsund (photograph on page 71).

Return to the original road and turn left to Fiskebäckskil where there is a ferry to *Lysekil* (**19**) which is one option for an overnight stay. Lysekil is a popular and old-established resort. There is plenty going on there: sailing, windsurfing, swimming, riding, concerts, dancing, golf and tennis. You can go on fishing excursions or take a boat trip to Smögen and some of the other coastal villages. The principal hotel is the Lysekil in the town centre while there is a nice camping site by the water and an attractive youth hostel. Lysekil would warrant a two night stay.

The alternative is to continue from Fiskebäckskil to the 161 where you turn right to *Uddevalla* (16 miles), passing the oldest church in the region at Bokenäs. There are some nice views of the Havstensfjord before you join the E6.

Uddevalla (**18**) is basically a commercial town and the principal industry was shipbuilding but the shipyard has now been closed. A very comfortable place to stay is the Bohusgården Hotel which has an elevated position on the southern edge of the town and which looks across the Byfjorden. It has recently been extended and has a restaurant, lounges, bar and a large indoor pool.

A left turn is necessary to drive up through a residential area to reach the hotel. If instead you continue along the main road and after about two miles take a right turn, you will come to *Gustavsberg*. This was a spa and Sweden's oldest seaside resort. It was mentioned by the notable Swedish botanist Carl von Linné in his book 'Westgötha Resa' (Travels in Västgöta) published in 1746. A number of the old buildings are preserved in delightful park-like surroundings, including the Societetsalongen – an elaborate wooden restaurant – while the original spa building is now a youth hostel.

DAY 5

Rejoin the E6 in the Oslo direction and shortly after Håby turn left on to roads 162/163 signed to Lysekil, Hamburgsund and Smögen. Keep to the 163 to Hamburgsund. If you stayed at Lysekil you will be on the 162 and need to turn left on to the 163 where the two roads meet.

You leave the 163 and follow the signs to *Kungshamn*, motoring through placid farming country but later coming to rocky tree-clad hills. As you approach Kungshamn there is an attractive camping site on the left by the water. Like all the villages along this stretch of coast it consists of a tight collection of colourful wooden houses. Kungshamn is a little larger than most and overlooking the harbour is the Hotel Kungshamn (60 rooms). Continue through the centre, and then take a sharp left which leads you up to a superb bridge which provides the link with *Smögen*. A car park on the right, just short of the bridge, gives you a wonderful view of the village and the immediate coastal area.

Smögen is most attractive with its cluster of little houses, the fishing boats and the rocky shoreline of smooth granite which has a pinkish tinge to it. Although this is a holiday area, commercial fishing is still very important as you will realise if you see the boats come in (incidentally fresh Smögen shrimps are renowned).

Return across the bridge (you will look across the Kungshamn on the right) and then turn left (marked to Dingle). The road goes through *Väjern*, another fishing village, past Hunnebostrand and Bovallstrand and when it reaches the 163 you turn left to *Hamburgsund*. Here you can take the ferry (five minutes) to Hamburgön and at the top of the Huseberget you will be rewarded with some splendid views. You keep to road 163 to *Grebbestad*, another pretty little place where the narrow road winds down to the water's edge.

The road then moves inland and at *Tanumshede* is the old-established Tanums Gestgifveri which is renowned for its food (for a full description see the Country Living itinerary). An ideal spot for a two night stay. If you wanted a bigger centre than you should join the E6 (once again) and 20 miles away is Strömstad where, in a prominent position, is the Hotel Laholmen, built in 1984 (one of the Reso chain). Strömstad, incidentally, claims to have more hours of sunshine than anywhere else in northern Europe.

DAY 6

There are several alternatives for your free day in Tanumshede. I would suggest you spend some time looking at the fascinating Bronze Age rock carvings which are at several locations in the immediate area (**20**). Those at Vitlycke are the most remarkable. Or you could make an excursion across the border into Norway (a day trip to Oslo is easily accomplished, and it takes about three hours to drive there). Or you could simply spend some time in gentle exploration of the attractive coastline and a glance at the map will indicate a number of possibilities.

DAY 7

Leave Tanumshede on the E6 (Gothenburg direction) and very shortly afterwards turn left on a secondary road to Naverstad. You will pass some of the rock carvings by the roadside near Fossum. When you reach road 165 turn left and at Bullarby turn right on road 164. The rolling countryside is enlivened by occasional glimpses of water. The next town is *Dals-Ed* which is to the left just off the main road. It is Dalsland's oldest tourist resort and lies between Lakes Stora Lee and Lilla Lee. There is a nice old wooden hotel here, the Carl XII. This area is fascinating for its sharp contrasts in scenery.

Where the 164 joins the 172 turn left and shortly afterwards take a minor road on the right to Dals Långed and continue along this byway, past the village of Tisselskog to *Håverud* (**22**). Part of this road is unsurfaced but it goes through some very enjoyable scenery.

On the approach to Håverud turn right (signed to Åsenbruk) and soon you cross the bridge high above the Dalsland Canal's aqueduct. Just beyond the bridge, on the left, is a car park. When you look down from the bridge (take your camera) there is, at a lower level, a railway bridge and below this the aqueduct carrying the canal and finally the surging rapids of the river Upperud. The aqueduct is combined with a triple lock and it was built in 1868. The designer was the noted Swedish engineer Nils Ericsson and he was responsible for the entire canal which is 158 miles long, has 29 locks and is considered to be one of the most beautiful waterways in the world. The aqueduct is 106 ft long, and the road bridge is 165 ft above the water.

Continue to Åsenbruk and turn right to Bäckefors along a switchback road which brings you to the 166 where you turn right. At Bäckefors turn left on to the 172 which takes you through a pleasant rural slice of Dalsland county until you join the E6 at Uddevalla and drive to *Gothenburg* (**17**). This is where you spend your final night in Sweden before returning to the UK.

THE LAKE VÄTTERN CIRCUIT

LAKE VÄTTERN IS Sweden's second largest lake and around its shores is a delightful mixture of sights and scenery. This itinerary takes you on a circuit of the lake, starting at Jönköping at its southern tip and going up the western side, first to the little resort of Hjo and then to the fortress town of Karlsborg. You spend three nights on this side of Vättern, so that you can explore the area before rounding the top of the lake, and then motoring south through Motala and the medieval town of Vadstena. You continue to picturesque Gränna which nestles on the lakeside, opposite the island of Visingsö and two nights are spent here, providing time for sightseeing or simply enjoying the surrounding scenery. There is also an opportunity for you to add on an excursion to Stockholm for one or two nights, or if you have children, to go and visit Kolmården zoo and safari park.

It is at this point, having almost completed a circuit of the lake, that you move east, first to Eksjö with its well preserved wooden houses and then to Växjö for your next overnight stop. Two places of major interest here are the Emigrants' House and the Glass Museum.

You now have the option of motoring direct to Gothenburg for your last night in Sweden, or breaking your journey on the west coast at Halmstad, or returning to the UK via Denmark with an overnight stop in Copenhagen.

This is an itinerary which includes several alternative excursions and the minimum number of nights in Sweden is seven, but eight or nine nights would give you more time to see this attractive area or it could easily be extended to 10 or 11 nights if you include Stockholm. *Maps 2 and 3.*

DAY 1

Leave Gothenburg on the E6, going south-east, but on the outskirts follow the signs to road 40 to Borås and Jönköping. You can use the signs to Gothenburg's Landvetter airport as an additional navigational aid as it lies to one side of road 40. This is a straightforward main road with nothing of particular interest. *Borås* is the centre of the 'weavers country' where Sweden's textile industry is based and if you want to pick up some bargains read the chapter on 'Shopping'. There is also a major zoo here with around 400 animals (**43**) ☆.

Jönköping (**47**) is a busy and attractive lakeside town where you should break your journey and visit the Swedish Match Museum which is in the original 1847 factory. There is also an extensive park where you get good views of the lake from the restaurant, the Värdshuset Stugan. South of the town even more striking views – taking in both Lake Vänern and Lake Vättern on a clear day – can be had from the top of Mt. Taberg. At Huskvarna, which is almost a continuation of Jönköping, you can meet the Swedish royal family at Dr. Skora's Waxworks (**49**) ☆.

Leave Jönköping on road 195 which parallels the lake and at

Hjo (**38**) follow the signs to the town centre. Hjo is one of my favourite places in this region, a small, older style lakeside resort which has retained some of its original atmosphere with its 19th century wooden houses and small harbour. You can tour the town sedately in a horse-drawn carriage or take a trip on an elderly 1892 steamer, somewhat prosaically called 'Trafik'. There is an aquarium and display of butterflies in the preserved Societethus in the park where the youth hostel occupies the Villa Eira. By the lake is a large open air swimming pool.

Right in the centre by the harbour and overlooking the lake is the modern Hotel Bellevue which has 100 bedrooms, a restaurant, taverna and café. It makes a good base for a two night stay (or longer) and is very comfortable.

DAY 2

Here are two suggestions for excursions. Leave Hjo on road 194 to Skövde, a commercial town of little interest, and continue on road 49 to *Skara* (**40**). The road climbs quite impressively to a high ridge of ground which forms a plateau about 1,000 ft above sea level and provides a panoramic view of Skövde and the surrounding countryside.

About five miles from Skara there is a right turn to Skara Sommarland which claims to be Scandinavia's largest activity park (**39**) ☆. There is no doubt about its size: it covers an area of 890,000 square yards and has over 70 attractions from lunar vehicles to water skiing (with a very good method of teaching children). It also has Europe's largest aqualand, is well laid out, has plenty of places to eat and offers entertainment by leading Swedish pop stars.

Skara has Sweden's oldest cathedral and also an interesting narrow-gauge museum railway. Follow the signs to Lidköping (**44**) where you can visit the old-established Rörstrand porcelain factory which has its own museum and shop. Rejoin the ring road around the town and follow the signs to *Läckö*. You drive through pretty countryside, where there are plenty of places where you can pause or have a picnic, to the tip of the Kållandsö peninsula where you will see the white bulk of Läckö Castle (**36**) ☆. Make a tour of the enormous number of rooms, look out over the beautiful lake and when you feel weary enjoy some excellent food in the castle restaurant or at the cafeteria just outside the walls. There are also interesting exhibitions held each year at the castle.

Return to the Lidköping ring road and join the 44 to Götene where it combines with the E3. Stay on this road until you see the signs to *Mariestad* and make a short visit to this pleasant lakeside town. Alternatively, take the secondary road, on the left, off the 44 at Skeby which follows the lake. At *Hällekis* you can see craftsmen working with wood, iron, linen and wool in the old mill and buy the finished products – as well as enjoying coffee and home-baked bread. When you leave, drive up the Kinnekulle, the local 'mountain' which is 1,000ft above sea level. This secondary road rejoins the E3/44 just a few miles from Mariestad.

When you leave Mariestad take road 48 to Skövde and then return to Hjo on the 194.

The alternative excursion repeats the first one as far as Skara, where you should follow the Falköping and Jönköping signs. At the former keep on the by-pass and when you reach a T-junction turn right and after a few hundred yards turn left on to a minor road to Åsle. You start with some impressive views across the countryside and the road then descends through Åsle and at Tiarp you take a sharp right turn when the road begins to climb quite steeply. At road 48, go straight across to *Tidaholm* (**41**) ☆.

This quiet town has a modest but interesting museum of industry and automobiles in the former Vulcan Match factory. The most interesting exhibits are the motor vehicles built by Tidaholms Bruk between 1903 and 1934. On the little island in the river Tidan, which flows through the town, is the old turbine house (Turbinhusön) which is now used for art exhibitions. Also on the island are four workers' cottages, two being completely furnished in 18th century style while another is devoted to handicrafts and the fourth is now a cosy little café with an open air terrace.

Leave on road 193 and then turn left on to road 47 signed to Jönköping, staying on this road until you reach a major roundabout with a motel at one side. Just beyond it look for a minor left turn marked to *Habo* church. The road becomes unsurfaced and wends its way across a serene rural landscape until you reach the church which is on the right hand side.

Habo (**42**) is one of the most remarkable timber churches in Sweden. Externally it is impressive, with its separate elegantly proportioned bell tower, but it is the interior which is quite staggering. Every part of the interior is painted with a representation of Luther's Catechism. The Ten Commandments are painted on the walls, even numbers on the north side, odd numbers on the south side. The Lord's Prayer is painted above the galleries while the Christian baptism and the Lord's Supper are on the ceiling of the nave where you will also find the Confession and Absolution. All this is the work of two men, Johan C. Peterson and Johan Kinnerus who completed it in only three years between 1741 and 1743. Also worthy of mention is the organ, made in 1731 by Johan Niclas Cahman, and which has a very beautiful organ case.

When you leave the village don't turn right to Jönköping, but keep straight on along another unsurfaced minor road which comes out on the 195 at Fiskebäck. Turn left and return to Hjo.

DAY 3

Leave Hjo on road 195 (northbound) which joins the 49 to *Karlsborg* (**37**) ☆ where you should explore the enormous fortress which was built between 1820 and 1909. It was intended to be the first of a pair which would form the central defence of Sweden, but by the time it was completed fortresses had gone out of fashion and the second one was never started. It has ramparts over three miles long, and a barrack block – the Slutvärnet – 2,224 ft long. Walls are over 6 ft thick and it required 250,000 tons of limestone which was ferried across from Omberg on the other side of the lake. It has an interesting museum and church. Parts of the fortress are still used as a training centre by the Swedish army.

Leaving Karlsborg you come to the bridge which crosses the Göta canal where it enters the lake. On the right hand side is the Kanalhotellet which is a suitable choice for an overnight stay (see Country Living for a longer description). If you haven't visited Mariestad you can make the excursion from Karlsborg, using road 202 and returning on 201. Or you could explore part of the Tiveden National Park with its extensive forests and many trails for walkers.

DAY 4

Go north on road 49 to Askersund which is worth a brief visit. Now you change direction going south on road 50 to *Motala* (**63**) ☆ which is where the Göta canal begins again and also where the Göta Canal Company has its offices. In the same building, which is by the harbour (parking nearby), is the interesting canal museum. In the market place is the statue to Baltzar von Platen, the creator of the canal who was also responsible for building the Karlsborg fortress. But the 58 locks were to the design of the great British engineer, Thomas Telford.

Stay on the 50 to *Vadstena* (**62**), one of only two genuine medieval towns in Sweden (the other being Visby on Gotland). The

town, which has a lovely lakeside location, is dominated by the castle which was begun in 1545 and is in Dutch renaissance style. The other major building is the Klosterkyrka, the 'blue church', which is early 15th century and made of limestone. It houses the relics of St Bridget (born 1303, died 1373 and canonised in 1391). Other historically interesting buildings in the town include the monastery, the convent, the 15th century courthouse, the medieval charity hospital and the old theatre. There are some well preserved streets and buildings.

Rejoin road 50 and then follow signs on the right to Borghamn where there is a very minor road over Omberg which rises, quite suddenly, some 580 ft above the lake. The road drops down the other side and you can return to road 50 after this worthwhile diversion. At Ödeshög turn right on to another minor road which goes through Uppgränna and then into *Gränna* (**55**), a picturesque little town facing the lake and backed by steep hills. Founded in 1652, it has been fortunate in avoiding the disastrous fires which have all too frequently destroyed Sweden's wooden towns in the past.

The Grännaberget, at the south east end of the town, is about 1,000 ft above sea level and provides a marvellous view of the lake. It can be reached by steps which start near the impressive church. Alternatively, drive under the E4 and soon after turn left on the road signed to the summit. There is an 88 ft high tower at the top of which is a splendid observation view.

There is a museum to S. A. Andrée, a native of Gränna, who in 1897 tried to fly over the North Pole in a balloon. The expedition failed and the remains of the balloon were found 33 years later and brought back to this little town. Gränna is also well known for its red and white peppermint rock (Polkagrisar) which has been made there since 1859. At the lakeside is the harbour and marina where the ferry sails to the island of Visingsö.

If you drive to the southern end of the town and instead of joining the E4 take a right turn along what was the old main road you will soon come to one of the more unusual hotels in Sweden, the Gyllene Uttern (Golden Otter). It looks like an old castle and has an interior to match but was in fact built only 50 years ago. It is now part of the Scandic chain and makes a good base for a two night stay. The restaurant is very good and the rooms well furnished, those overlooking the lake having a splendid view. There is even a wedding chapel at the hotel.

DAY 5

On your 'free' day you could make a visit to Visingsö (**56**) or visit Linköping or just indulge in some quiet exploration in the immediate area. Crossing to *Visingsö* takes 20 minutes on the ferry and one way of seeing the island is by horse-drawn cart, which is called a Remmalag. You should make a point of seeing the baroque parish church with its separate bell tower which was built on the orders of Per Brahe, Count of Visingsö. By the harbour are the remains of Visingsborg Castle which was burnt down in 1718, while the remains of Näs Castle, built in 1150, are at the south end of the island.

Take the E4 to *Linköping* (**65**) ☆ where the biggest attraction is the wonderful open air museum. It gives you a very good idea of how a Swedish provincial town would have looked in the late 19th century. There are 80 buildings and they have been re-erected in the same street pattern as that of old Linköping. It is also unusual in that there are at least 50 permanent residents in the town which makes it more alive than many similar open air museums. There are several craftsmen's workshops and the many buildings include shops, a bank, the school house, an old ropeworks and an early chocolate factory. There is an inn which is in full working order.

Linköping has strong associations with the Swedish aircraft industry and aviation enthusiasts should see the Air Force Museum with its unique collection of old aircraft (some of them being British designs). It is at Malmslätt on the outskirts. The Cathedral with its impressive spire, 350 ft high, has Romanesque and Gothic features and was built by stonemasons from England and France as well as Sweden.

Return to Gränna via Berg (**64**) to see the Göta Canal locks, keeping to the minor road through Ljungsbro. Shortly afterwards it becomes delightfully rural all the way to Borensberg. Here you will see the only remaining manually controlled locks, while a few hundred yards away is an old hotel, the Göta Canal Värdshus, where you can sit outside and watch any canal traffic that may be passing. From Borensberg join road 36 to Motala and then the 50 to Ödeshög and back to Gränna.

There are two additonal excursions you can add on to the itinerary at this stage. One is to Stockholm (taking the E4 all the way) and staying one or two nights, and the other – if you have children – is to Kolmården zoo and safari park (**66**) ☆. Again you take the E4 via Linköping and Norrköping and a few miles beyond the latter turn right to Getå and Kolmården. The zoo is large and imaginatively laid out and has over 1,000 animals. The safari park is also extensive while there is a dolphinarium, an adventure land for children and a cable car system which makes a circuit of the entire area. There is also a large modern hotel – the Vildmarks Hotellet – which overlooks Bråviken Bay.

DAY 6

Leave Gränna on the 133 to Säby, where you turn right on to the 32 to *Eksjö* (**54**). This attractive little town with its market square and streets of old wooden buildings is well worth a short visit. Call at the tourist office for details of the route to be walked and the old houses to be seen. Eksjö is also a military town and the former base of the

Hussar Regiment whose museum is open to visitors. Alternatively, go south on the E4 almost to Jönköping and then turn left on to the 31/33 and at Riddersberg (50) ☆ go and see the remarkable wooden sculptures of artist Calle Örnemark. Afterwards continue on the 33 to Eksjö.

Motor south on the 32 to Vetlanda, then continue on the 31 and a little way beyond Norrhult take a right turn on the 23 to *Växjö* (53). Historically this town was an important trading and ecclesiastical centre and the first church was established here in the 11th century by an English missionary. Today the two buildings which are of particular interest are the Emigrants' House, a permanent exhibition relating to the emigration of Swedes to America, and the Småland Museum which includes the glass museum.

Only 30–40 miles to the east is the 'Kingdom of Glass' (59) where glassworks bearing such famous names as Boda, Kosta and Orrefors are to be found. An extra night at Växjö would give you adequate time to explore this area.

There are numerous hotels in Växjö, although I don't have any personal knowledge of them. The biggest hotel in the centre is the Statt (one of the Sara chain) while on the outskirts are two modern motels, a Scandic and an OK Motorhotell.

DAY 7

You can either go straight to Gothenburg (17) for your last night in Sweden before returning to the UK or you can go to the west coast and spend a night at Halmstad. A third option is to go south to Helsingborg and across to Denmark, spending one night in Copenhagen before returning to Britain from the port of Esbjerg.

For Gothenburg leave Växjö on road 25, briefly join the E4 near Ljungby, then bear right on to the 25 again all the way to the E6. Turn right and you are on a straight course to Gothenburg. If you are staying at Halmstad take the same route to the E6 and then follow the signs into the town. For a description of Halmstad (10) see 'Along the West Coast'.

If you go for option three, when you get to the E4 stay on it all the way to Helsingborg, cross the Sound to Helsingør in Denmark (ferry takes 25 minutes, frequent sailings). Copenhagen is 27 miles from Helsingør and Esbjerg is 174 miles from the Danish capital (but don't forget the 50 minute ferry crossing between Zealand and Funen).

If you have children there is one last attraction I would mention and that is High Chaparral (51) ☆ which is the American Wild West Swedish style – the brainchild of Big Bengt Erlandsson. To find it, leave Växjö on the 25, bear right on the 27 to Värnamo and continue on the same road where it crosses the E4. At Kärda turn right and you will, in due course, see High Chaparral. Here you can ride the stage, watch a shoot-out, visit the Indian reservation, travel on a steam train which is waylaid by outlaws, visit an incredible museum which has everything from a locomotive to the contents of a village store, or sail on the Mexican Queen. You can also eat and drink, ride a pony, and go shopping or panning for gold. You will either like it or hate it; most children love it.

Return to Kärda, turn right and stay on the 27 to Bradaryd then on the 153 all the way to the E6 at Varberg, then turn right to Gothenburg. For option two leave the 153 at Skeppshult and continue on the 26 to the E6 at Halmstad. For option three turn left at Kärda and rejoin the E4 turning right to go south to Helsingborg.

COAST, COUNTRY, ÖLAND AND GLASS

As this itinerary concentrates on south east Sweden, you can conveniently travel via Denmark, making the short ferry crossing over the Sound which separates the two countries. Your first destination is Jönköping at the southern tip of Lake Vättern, after which it is the 'Kingdom of Glass' that beckons. You drive through this area in which the majority of Swedish glassworks are located on your way to the fine old town of Kalmar with its magnificent castle.

Now comes the exploration of the attractive island of Öland which is linked to the Swedish mainland by Europe's longest bridge. Öland has its own distinctive landscape and is also noted for its wooden windmills – 400 of them.

Returning to the mainland your route is south, keeping to the coast to visit the naval town of Karlskrona and then moving inland through Kristianstad to the old university and cathedral town of Lund. After stopping here it is back to the coast and across to Denmark for your return journey to Britain.

You can complete this itinerary with nine nights in Sweden but I would suggest you stay at least 10 nights, or longer if you want to loiter on the island of Öland. You can also very easily have a night in Copenhagen, either on your outward or return journey. *Map 1.*

DAY 1

Having arrived at Esbjerg from Britain, you motor across Jutland and the island of Funen on the E66. You have a 50 minute break from driving while you are ferried across the Great Belt separating the islands of Funen and Zealand. As you approach Copenhagen follow the E4 signs to Helsingør which is where you take the ferry for the 25 minute crossing to Helsingborg. Of course if you decide to stay overnight in wonderful Copenhagen, you should follow the signs to the centre from the E66/E4.

As it is likely that you will arrive at Helsingborg (**1**) in the evening, it is a natural choice for your first overnight stop. There is a wide range of hotels in the town centre with others on the outskirts.

DAY 2

Leave Helsingborg on the clearly signed E4. After about 12 miles, at Åstorp, you turn right on to road 21 to *Klippan* (**3**) ☆ where there is the Silver Hill Aircraft and Motor Museum which also has Lipizzaner horses. Another attraction at Klippan is a preserved railway which runs to Ljungbyhed. Continue to where road 108 intersects the 21 and turn left, driving via Oderljunga to Åsljunga where you turn right rejoining the E4.

The E4 cuts through pleasant, if not exceptional, farming country. You by-pass Ljungby and at *Lagan* there is a motor museum (**52**) ☆, in which the 30 or so vehicles have all been lovingly restored by the owner, Alf Johansson (and they are all runners). You can take a left turn here and go along a minor road to the shores of the Bolmen lake, a beautiful area, and at Tannåker there is access to the island of Bolmsö. To return to the E4 drive via Dannäs (turn right and left), bearing right at Årved to Värnamo.

If you ignored this diversion you would have driven alongside Lake Vidöstern and beyond Dörarp there is an attractive hotel, Toftaholm, on the left (for details see Country Living). If you have children with you then there is another excursion you can make, this time to High Chaparral (**51**) ☆, Sweden's Wild West extravaganza. Turn left on to road 27 at Värnamo and five miles later at Kärda turn right and in due course you will come to High Chaparral. On leaving, continue on the same road, turn right to Hillerstorp and then keep to a minor road through Uppebo to Skillingaryd when you can join the E4.

If the Swedish idea of the Wild West doesn't appeal, then turn right on to the 27 near Värnamo and about five miles later you will come to *Bor* where you should turn left on to a minor road to Gälleryd and Os. Here there is something for the train enthusiast, the Ohs Bruk narrow-gauge museum railway, a former industrial line built in 1907 (**60**) ☆.

Rail enthusiast or not, you turn right at Os and at a minor crossroads turn left to Nydala. The immediate area is hilly with Lake Rusken on the left and some beautiful views. At Nydala turn left on to the 27 and almost immediately turn right on to a minor road which joins the 30 near *Hok*. Just beyond the village is Hook Manor Hotel on the right which would make an excellent choice for a night stop (for details see Country Living). If you don't stay at Hok then Jönköping would be the alternative in which case continue on the 30 until it joins the E4 (where you will be if you have ignored my suggested diversions).

Jönköping (**47**) is a busy town on Lake Vättern with an interesting Match Museum, a very nice park and some good viewpoints.

DAY 3

From Jönköping join roads 31/33 to the east of the town. Less than five miles along this road you will see a minor road on the right to *Riddersberg* where you will find the home and studio of the Swedish sculptor Calle Örnemark (**50**) ☆. You can't miss it because in the distance you will see Örnemark's 338 ft high Indian rope-trick, the world's tallest wooden statue. This is just a foretaste of the other astonishing wooden sculptures of this talented artist, one of them being an incredible full-scale interpretation of the Mutiny on the Bounty. There are many more smaller exhibits in the grounds which you are free to wander round. Don't miss seeing Örnemark's work. If you have stayed at Hok you can cut a corner by taking the road via Ödestugu and Tenhult where you turn left on to the 31/33 and will see Riddersberg on the left.

Two other places of interest in the environs of Jönköping are Dr. Skora's Waxworks Museum at Huskvarna (**49**)|☆|and the

93

Gunsmith's Museum and Handicraft Centre at Smedbyn.

Continue on the 31/33 and at Nässjö you keep to the 31 through Vetlanda towards Kalmar. Beyond Lenhovda you should keep to the 31 if you wish to visit *Orrefors* Glassworks or alternatively bear right on the 123 if you want to see Kosta or Boda Glassworks. At Orrefors you turn left and you will find the glassworks on the left. It is highly organised to handle visitors and you can go on a conducted tour, seeing the various glass-making processes, while there is a permanent exhibition and museum, a large shop selling reduced price 'seconds', and a very good cafeteria and restaurant.

If you take road 123 you will see the *Kosta* works on the left. This is the oldest glassworks in Sweden having been established in 1743. At Kosta there is an exhibition hall and museum, a shop, the Kosta Inn and a camping site. Continue to Eriksmåla and turn left on to the 25 and after about eight miles you will see a sign to *Boda* on the left. Boda is another famous glassmaker and within this area there are around 100 glassworks, many being open to visitors and having shops selling their products.

Resume your journey on the 25; this bypasses Nybro and joins the 31 (from Orrefors) to *Kalmar* (**58**). I have allowed two nights in Kalmar so that you can explore this interesting town or the surrounding area – you may wish to make a further excursion around the 'Kingdom of Glass'.

There are a number of hotels in Kalmar, including the Stadshotell which occupies a rather splendid building in the town centre just near the cathedral. The interior is completely modernised while the restaurant – the Queen Victoria – is excellent. I can also recommend the Slottshotellet which has a quiet location beside the park, near the castle. The hotel was built in 1864 and is surrounded by 17th and 18th century buildings. The decor is in keeping with the building while you take breakfast or evening coffee in a charming little pavilion with a terrace outside. There is no restaurant but you don't have to go far to find one. The hotel has its own parking area. Other hotels include the Scandic (outside the town) and the Witt (one of the Sara chain).

DAY 4

The most notable building in Kalmar is the castle and it is well worth a visit with its many fine rooms (I found the Lozenge Hall, completed around 1580, one of the most fascinating with its intarsia decoration). There is also a separate exhibition within the castle devoted to the royal warship 'Kronan' which was designed in 1665 by an Englishman, Francis Sheldon. The vessel was sunk by accident when preparing to do battle with the Danish and Dutch fleets in 1676. The wreck was located in 1980 and many items have now been raised from the sea bed and restored and are to be seen in this well arranged exhibition.

The town is very old-established and has had links with commerce, shipping and fishing for centuries. The centre is almost on an island – Kvarnholmen – and in the main square are the merchants' houses and the cathedral, the biggest baroque church in Sweden (built 1660 – 1703). The empire style city hall and the Guild House in Dutch style are two other noteworthy buildings. Around this area is a fortified wall and the town gates. There is also an interesting maritime museum and an art museum.

If you have time to spare after seeing the town you may want to visit more glassworks or you can drive on road 25 to Lessebo (**57**) where there is a paper mill which continues to make paper by hand as they did 300 years ago. There are guided tours of the works.

DAY 5

Leave Kalmar and cross the longest bridge in Europe (19,914 ft in length) to the island of Öland, 87 miles long and 10 miles wide. More details of the island will be found in the separate chapter on Gotland and Öland.

Follow the signs to *Borgholm* (road 136), the largest town. The landscape is a mixture of treeless plain (in the south) and the forested areas (in the north) and is generally flat or gently undulating. Immediately noticeable are the distinctive wooden windmills. Originally there were 2,000 of them and 400 have been preserved.

On your way to Borgholm you will see on the left Halltorps Gästgiveri, which is renowned for its food. Not only is the cuisine of a high standard but the food is served in delightful surroundings. There is a good wine list. Although primarily a restaurant there are 10 comfortable rooms.

Halltorps is five miles from Borgholm and before you reach the town you will see the imposing ruins of the castle on the left.

Below it and looking towards the Kalmar Sound is Solliden (**121**), the royal summer residence, built 1903 – 1906. The park is open to the public. Borgholm (**120**) is a pleasant, if unexceptional, town which makes a satisfactory base for exploring the island and I have suggested a two night stay here. The principal hotel is the Strand with 135 bedrooms, several restaurants, a disco, a piano bar and a large indoor pool with sauna, solarium and exercise room. Bedrooms are well furnished and many of them overlook the sea. Although there are comparatively few hotels on the island there are plenty of camping sites, including some large ones in the north.

DAY 6

Although most visitors will want to indulge in some gentle exploration, for the more energetic it is quite feasible to make a complete circuit of the island in a day. Here is a run down of some of the places you will see. Start by going north from Borgholm on the 136 passing *Föra* with its large village church with a well-preserved medieval fortified tower. There are many of these fortified churches on the island. Go off to the left to *Sandvik* on the coast where there is an impressive windmill (now a restaurant) and take a right turn just before you reach the harbour. This is a rather rough minor road that keeps to the coast and you can see where the limestone has been quarried out of the cliffs. On the cliff edge is a very distinctive windmill which was used for polishing the stone. The road turns inland and if you bear right at Sörbyn you will emerge on to the 136.

Getting near the northern end of the island it is forested, while at *Böda* there are large camping sites and a sandy beach. The beach which curves round Böda Bay is regarded as the best on the island but it is quite narrow. At the northern tip is *Grankullavik* where you can see the Långe Erik lighthouse. You have now changed direction and are moving south on the west coast. At *Byxelkrok* there is a little harbour and shingle beach and the granite domed island of Blå Jungfrun (the Blue Maiden) is visible in the distance. It is a national park and can be visited.

Before you get back to Böda again, turn right to *Byerums Raukar* with its pleasant little beach fringed with trees. Where the road swings inland it passes Hornsviken, the island's only lake. At Köping turn left to *Egby* instead of keeping to the main road to Borgholm. This secondary road goes right down the eastern side of the island. Egby has the smallest church on the island while that at *Gärdslösa* (**124**) is particularly fine with 17th and 18th century frescoes and decorations. Between Egby and Gärdslösa there is a row of seven windmills – the largest group on Öland (**122**). But the row of five windmills at *Lerkaka Kvarnar* is, in my opinion, more photogenic (see photograph on page 71). At *Långlöt* there is the Himmelsberga Hembygds museum which is worth a short stop.

The road goes through a succession of villages, each with their substantial church, and at Gårdby you reach the beginning of the

Stora Alvaret, a treeless plain, 25 miles long, where the limestone often comes to the surface. Beyond Segerstad look out for the Solgården, a completely isolated, but very pleasant, little hotel. It lies on the left hand side and makes a good lunch or refreshment stop. At *Gräsgård* you can turn left and go down to the little fishing harbour while beyond the village watch for the right turn to Eketorps Borg (**123**), the reconstruction of a 5th century fortress which has an interesting museum within its walls.

At Ottenby (**126**) turn left on to the road through the nature reserve (popular with birdwatchers) which leads to the southern tip of the island where the tall Långe Jan lighthouse acts as a marker. The southern half of Öland may be flat and rather desolate but it has a distinct atmosphere of its own.

You now turn north, keeping to the west side of the island. Near *Grönhögen* there is one end of Karl Gustav's wall which was built in 1650 and stretches across the island. It kept the deer in for the king's hunting pleasure and the peasantry out so they couldn't poach the royal game. Beyond Torslunda you are back to the approach road to the bridge and you continue on the 136 back to Borgholm.

DAY 7

Drive across the bridge to the mainland and on to the ring road around Kalmar keeping to the E66 south to Karlskrona..

Karlskrona (**61**) is the Swedish equivalent of Plymouth or Portsmouth, being a town with long established naval connections. The centre of the town is on an island, and just off the main square is the Statt Hotel which makes a luxurious overnight base. Although it occupies a classic turn of the century building the interior has been completely redecorated, with sumptuously furnished bedrooms. There is a high class restaurant, the Carolus, a relaxing piano bar and Charlies, an elegant and swinging nightclub. Obviously the Statt isn't cheap but it does have high standards. Alternatives are the OK Motorhotell, the Savoy and the Siesta. The Statt doesn't have its own car park, but if you get a ticket at reception you can leave your car in the underground car park of the nearby department store – but remember that it is closed overnight.

DAY 8

You could easily spend an extra night in Karlskrona, leaving you a free day to explore this very interesting town. There is, in particular, a wonderful naval museum with a comprehensive and fascinating range of exhibits including a splendid gallery of ships' figureheads. Also of interest is the Admiralitetskyrkan, one of the oldest wooden churches in Sweden (1680), and in the main square there are two quite different churches designed by the same architect. One is the Trinity or German Church and the other Frederik's Church, named after King Frederik 1. The Blekinge county museum in Grevagården, a 1705 mansion, and the old shipyard are two other places of interest. You can also take a boat trip around the archipelago.

On leaving Karlskrona you rejoin the E66 south which by-passes the coastal towns which include Ronneby Brunn, a famous spa in the last century and which is now a major conference and recreation centre; and Karlshamn, which was renowned in the 1800's for the manufacture of snaps (aquavit), punch and tobacco. The Mörrum river which enters the sea at Karlshamn is famous for its salmon, the record weight for a fish being 52lb. At Sölvesborg, the narrow streets and old buildings reflect its medieval origins and on the nearby island of Hanö there is an English cemetery dating from the Napoleonic wars.

The E66 now moves inland and it is worth leaving it for a brief visit to Kristianstad (9), on the Helge river, which was a fortress town established by King Christian IV in 1614. The main square is surrounded by buildings of classical appearance while the Trinity Church is a beautiful renaissance design with a magnificent organ facade. An unusual museum is that devoted to the Swedish film industry. It houses the country's oldest recording studio which was in use between 1909 and 1911. Early Swedish films are on video tape and can be seen on request. There is also an interesting railway museum, the town at one time being a busy junction.

The main road continues through farming country until you need to turn off to enter *Lund* (6), one of Sweden's oldest towns. Established in 1020 by King Canute, it had become the spiritual and cultural centre of northern Europe by 1100. It is not the easiest town to drive around as there are numerous narrow streets, some of which have limited access for motor vehicles, and parking places are also rather restricted.

I have suggested a two night stay in Lund so that there is adequate time to explore the town. Hotels in the centre include the Grand, Lundia and Concordia. The latter is tucked away in a small, quiet street but very close to the centre and with a public car park just round the corner. Completely modernised inside, it is convenient and comfortable. It doesn't have a restaurant but there are plenty in the town centre and one that I can recommend is Stäket, only five minutes' walk away.

DAY 9

Any tour of Lund must begin with the cathedral which was consecrated in 1145 and is considered to be the finest Romanesque building in Scandinavia. The most fascinating feature of the interior is the 14th century astronomical clock which 'performs' at noon (1.00p.m. on Sundays) and 3.00p.m. every day. There are magnificent choir stalls and a beautiful altar piece from the 15th century; the crypt is also most impressive.

Next in importance is Kulturen which is an open air museum, in the centre of the town, with a collection of 30 old buildings all of which have been carefully re-erected on the site. They even include a farm complete with some animals. The museum's exhibits are wide-ranging and include among others, porcelain, silverware and textiles. You can wander round the museum and the grounds, visit the cafeteria or make some purchases at the turn of the century grocery shop.

Lund University was founded in 1666 so there are many buildings connected with this seat of learning, dating from the 17th century to the present day. There are museums covering art, zoology, history and the cathedral.

If historical towns are not to your taste you can drive along the E66 north, and then after about 18 miles bear left on the 23 to *Höör*. This road goes between two lakes and on the right hand side you will see a sign to Bosjökloster (7), which was originally a Benedictine convent founded in 1080. At Höör (8) ☆ take a left turn to Frostavallen, Skåne's biggest recreation area. There are miles of marked trails, a lakeside beach, a zoo, a reconstruction of a stone age settlement and a children's playground. You can hire a bike or boat or fish in the lake. There is also an hotel, restaurant, cafeteria and youth hostel.

There is some attractive scenery in the area around Höör and Frostavallen while this part of Skåne has many castles and manor houses.

DAY 10

Drive to Malmö on the E66, follow the ring road signs to Limhamn for the ferry to Dragør in Denmark (crossing time 50 minutes, reservation recommended). If you are returning to Esbjerg direct, you will need to catch the 9.35 a.m. ferry from Limhamn to give yourself adequate time for the journey. After leaving the ferry, drive through Dragør and follow the signs to the E4 (Sud) which takes you round Copenhagen. Later you must watch for the E66 signs and keep on this road across Zealand and, after crossing the Great Belt, over Funen and Jutland to Esbjerg.

Alternatively you can cross over to Denmark and follow the signs into the centre of Copenhagen if you are spending a night in the Danish capital. In this case you could always spend some time in *Malmö* (5) before taking the ferry. It has an interesting collection of museums and a castle, while you can get a bird's eye view of the city and the surrounding area from the top of the 253 ft high Hyllie water tower.

TO THE ARCTIC CIRCLE

THIS IS THE BIG ONE – the long haul to northern Sweden, but well worth the effort because the scenery is magnificent. You also see a great deal of Sweden: farmland, forest, mountains, lakes, rivers and coastline. Starting from Gothenburg your first stop is around Filipstad and then it is on to the folklore county of Dalarna and the beautiful area around Lake Siljan. The next stage of this northern journey brings you to Östersund in the centre of Sweden and another lakeland region. Here you can add on an excursion to Åre before continuing north to meet an increasingly impressive landscape with fewer signs of habitation. There is a visit to Arjeplog, surrounded by glittering lakes and with a backdrop of distant mountains.

This is Lapland, where you must watch for wandering reindeer. After an overnight stop at Arvidsjaur you cross the magic Arctic Circle at Jokkmokk and travel on to Gällivare where you can stay on the Dundret mountain. After a week of motoring you are now within reach of your final destination. Your route takes you through some of Europe's most spectacular scenery and along the impressive new road to your journey's end just short of the Norwegian frontier.

You can make an excursion to the Norwegian port of Narvik before embarking on your return journey which takes you through Kiruna to Luleå on the Gulf of Bothnia. Here you have an easy option: to take the Swedish State Railways' car sleeper train all the way to Gothenburg. If you keep on motoring it is a case of following the east coast through Skellefteå, Umeå, the stunning High Coast area around Kramfors, Härnösand and Sundsvall to the quiet little town of Järvsö.

The route south continues through Bollnäs to Gävle where you can either go to Uppsala and Stockholm or alternatively motor direct to Gothenburg.

Although the total mileage of this itinerary is considerable, the daily runs can be accomplished without difficulty and still leave time to absorb your surroundings and stop off at places of interest. But you need a minimum of 14 days for the trip and 16 – 18 days would be much more preferable. *Maps 1, 2, 3, 4, 5, 6/7, 8/10 and 9.*

DAY 1

On leaving the Gothenburg ferry terminal follow the E6 signs to begin with but then watch for those to road 45. You will go through a tunnel and over a viaduct high above the river (and the E6). On the opposite side you will turn right which looks as though you are heading back to Gothenburg, but don't panic, watch the signs carefully and you will swing right round and descend to road 45 on the opposite bank of the river to the E6.

The first part of the 45 is through quite gentle farmland, bypassing Trollhättan, going through Vänersborg and keeping broadly parallel to Lake Vänern. You also bypass Karlstad when you leave the 45/E18 and choose road 63 which takes you through more interesting and changeable scenery to *Filipstad*. This is your first overnight stop, about 185 miles from Gothenburg. There is a convenient Scandic hotel in the town centre or you can stay just outside at the attractive Hennickehammar Herrgård (see Country Living). A third alternative is to continue on the 63 to Hammarn and then turn right to Grythyttan and stay at the delightful Grythyttans Gästgivaregård (also described in Country Living).

DAY 2

Wherever you have stayed you need to be on the 63 which continues through Hallefors to Kopparberg (**76**), once the centre of the mining industry and which now has several interesting museums and is worth a short stop.

A call at *Grängesberg* (**86**) ☆ is only necessary if you are a railway enthusiast because as you approach the town there is a left turn signed to the railway museum (Grängesbergs Lokmuseum) whose collection includes two highly unusual steam turbine locomotives.

Ludvika and Borlänge are both industrial and commercial centres but at the latter, if you stay on road 60, you can make a deviation to *Falun* (**85**), 12 miles away; otherwise follow the 70/71 signs. Falun was the centre of the copper mining industry and at one time two thirds of the world's copper was extracted from the 'big hole'. You can see the old mine and visit the interesting museum devoted to the development of the industry. Leave Falun on the 293 and you will meet up with roads 70/71 where you turn right.

This is Dalarna county, one of the most attractive regions of Sweden and a popular holiday area. *Leksand* (**88**), on one arm of Lake Siljan is a sunny little town with an open air museum and an impressive church and well worth a short stop. When you leave, keep to the secondary road beside the lake, passing a good camping site and also a children's Sommarland. The road has many twists and turns and you will pass several small craft workshops while at Hjortnäs there is the intriguing Tin Museum (Tennfigur Museum) (**89**) ☆ with its displays and dioramas featuring thousands of miniature metal figures.

Tällberg enjoys a lovely position overlooking the lake and has numerous hotels. If you want a short break from driving stop off at the Klockargården – a combination of hotel, café and a shop selling tasteful handicrafts (for more details see Delightful Dalarna and Värmland).

You now rejoin the 70 (turn left) and pass Rättvik (**90**) and after about 16 miles look for a left turn to *Nusnäs* (**91**) ☆. When you come to the village watch for an abrupt right (signed Dalahäst – tillverkning) which brings you to the workshops where they make the famous brightly painted wooden Dalecarlia horses. Carving and painting horses began in Dalarna in the 19th century and this is the only place that these well-known Swedish souvenirs are made.

After rejoining the 70 you are soon on the outskirts of *Mora* (**92**), the biggest town on Lake Siljan and a major holiday centre. This is an obvious choice for an overnight stop while two nights would give you more time to explore the immediate area. You can, for example, go round the lake, drive up the Gesunda mountain (1,686 ft above sea level), have a look at the little island of Sollerön or take a trip on the lake. Part way up Gesunda mountain is a children's attraction, Santaworld (**93**) ☆.

In the centre of Mora is the Mora Hotel which makes a comfortable overnight base, while other hotels include the Ljustret and the Scandic (on the outskirts).

DAY 3

Leave Mora on road 81, starting alongside Lake Orsa before going through some enjoyable rolling countryside. At the small town of Sveg you join road 312 and after about eight miles make a right turn on to a well-surfaced secondary road, a short cut through extensive forests to *Vemdalen* where you turn right on to the 315. From Vemdalen the road climbs quite steeply between forest and mountains which rise up to 3,300 ft above sea level. Part way up on the left hand side is a small, unpretentious little café which produced a satisfying and inexpensive lunch when I passed that way. The road reaches a high plateau, at the end of which there are some fine views on the right.

When the road splits you keep to the 316 through Klövsjö and Åsarne where it joins the 81 to *Östersund* (**105**). There are some fine views of the lakes and eventually the road parallels Lake Storsjön to Östersund. This is the largest town in central Sweden and is 522 miles from Gothenburg and 528 miles from Kiruna. Have a look at Jamtli, the fascinating open air museum where you can see people living and working as they did in the 18th and 19th centuries. It is one of Sweden's largest museums of this kind. Drive across to the island of Frösön (**106**) with its well kept 12th century church and 18th century bell tower. From the highest point on the island you get a wonderful view across the lake to the distant mountains. The island also has a rather exciting looking golf course. The lake is said to possess a monster so you can look for it if you take one of the regular cruises on the veteran steamship Thomée. Hotels in the town include the Britannia, Jämteborg, Scandic, Winn (a Sara hotel), Zäta and Östersund. If you are extending the basic itinerary then a two night stay would be worthwhile or alternatively you could spend one night here and one night at *Åre* (**102**).

Åre is more a winter sports centre than a summer resort, but the superb scenery is there at all seasons of the year. Leave Östersund on the E75 and instead of going direct you can turn right beyond

Krokom and use the secondary road via Nälden and Alsen. This provides some lovely views to the left before you rejoin the E75 at Morsil and continue to Åre. The town faces the Åresjön lake while behind it looms the bulk of mount Åreskutan, 4,658 ft above sea level. You can take a cable car to just below the summit and then walk to the top. There is also a mountain railway which goes from the town centre as far as Mörvikshummeln.

A more ambitious excursion is to continue beyond Åre on the E75, crossing the Norwegian frontier, and then turning right on to road 72, re-entering Sweden shortly afterwards. The 72 keeps alongside Lake Kallsjön, through Kall, and rejoins the E75 at Järpen, where you turn left to go to Östersund or right to return to Åre. There are several hotels at Åre and I had a comfortable stay at the Åregården. There is also a lakeside camping site here and a youth hostel (five miles east of the town on the E75).

When you return on the E75 to Östersund, watch for the small right turn before Halland which will take you to the Rista waterfall (**104**), an impressive sight (photograph on page 111). There is only a camping site sign on the road and this is, in fact, right beside the falls – which is fine if you don't mind the sound of running water.

DAY 4

After leaving Östersund on road 88 you are soon aware of the increasing emptiness of the landscape with less habitation and more extensive views. At Strömsund, an uninteresting town, reached over an impressive bridge you join a sparsely inhabited area, while at Lövberga there is a good view along Lake Flåsjön. Continue through Hoting (car museum on the outskirts) (**101**) ☆ to *Dorotea* by which time you will have crossed into the vast county of Lapland.

On the northern outskirts of Dorotea, on the left, is the excellent Hotel Dorotea which you could use as your overnight stop, or alternatively merely call in for a meal. There is a cafeteria and a restaurant and the hotel is well-known for its food. Östersund to Dorotea is 114 miles.

Beyond Dorotea the landscape is rather flat until you reach *Vilhelmina*, 35 miles away. It lies on a hillside and has, in the centre, the original church village – the wooden houses now providing accommodation for tourists. At the highest point is the impressive wooden church.

From Vilhelmina it is a further 43 miles to Storuman, a town of little interest but a useful overnight stop as it has a reasonable hotel, the Toppen, which is on the right hand side of the road in the town centre.

DAY 5

Your northward journey continues on the 343, the scenery being a succession of trees, rocks and water; about the only village of any size is Sorsele. When you reach Slagnäs, turn left half way through the village, to *Arjeplog* (36 miles). Don't take the earlier turn before Slagnäs which is a *very* minor road and rather rough.

The secondary road you take is very scenic and well-surfaced all the way to Arjeplog (**111**) ☆, which enjoys a marvellous position between Lakes Hornavan and Uddjaure and is, in fact, almost surrounded by water. This small town lies on the 'silver road', a historic route from Skellefteå on the Gulf of Bothnia to Bodø on the coast of Norway and became a modern highway as recently as 1974. One reason for the diversion to Arjeplog is to visit the fascinating Silver Museum which has a unique collection of Lappish silver as well as an incredible range of other exhibits relating to the Lapps and their history in this remote region. This quite remarkable museum was established by the equally remarkable Einar Wallqvist, who is known as the Doctor of the Lapps. Although he is now of a considerable age, Dr. Wallqvist is still very active and is also an

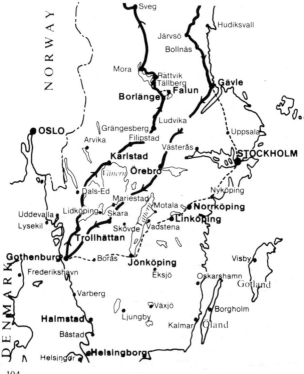

accomplished author, artist and linguist as well as the curator of this museum. A visit is not to be missed on any account. High above the town is the Silverhatten Hotel which, in spite of its northern location, includes an outdoor tennis court among its amenities. On the outskirts of the town at Kraja is a large, and attractively located, camping site which stretches down to one of the lakes and has a restaurant in the old Krajagården inn.

From Arjeplog take road 373/95 to *Arvidsjaur* but after about two miles take a minor road on the left which goes up to the summit of Galtisbuouda (it is signed to Natur Reservat and Galtisbuouda) (**113**). Keep your eyes open because you take a sharp right and then a left turn. The road is surfaced almost all the way, while the final section, up to a radio transmitter at the summit (2,624 ft above sea level) is rough but well worth the effort. The views all round are spectacular: lakes like silver, and mountains stretching to infinity,

layer after layer of them, each successive range changing in colour. Another little excursion which shouldn't be missed.

Return to road 375/95 and continue to Arvidsjaur (**114**), a remarkably busy place, part of its activity being explained by the fact that it is an army training centre for Swedish conscripts (they have a modern barracks on the outskirts). The town has grown up over the last 100 years and was originally a small trading post. You can see a traditional Lapp settlement here with tent-shaped wooden huts called Kåtor and also Härbren – the distinctive wooden storehouses. These buildings are still used from time to time by the Same people which is the 'real' name of the Lapps. For an overnight stay I can recommend the modern Hotel Laponia which provides excellent food and very comfortable rooms and has a friendly staff. It is almost on the outskirts and near an attractive camping site. The latter also has some modern chalets, these being let to holiday-makers in summer and used by the conscripts in winter.

DAY 6

Some 97 miles from Arvidsjaur on road 343 is the Arctic Circle and in between there is very little except for an abundance of wonderful scenery which emphasises the vastness of this part of Sweden. Just short of *Jokkmokk* (**115**) there is a sign on the right marking the Arctic Circle and if you want permanent proof of having 'crossed the line' go up to the Polar Circle Fish Camp just above the road where you can have a certificate with your name on it for Skr10.

Jokkmokk – it means a 'bend in the stream' in the Lapp language – is the only town of any size in the kommun of the same name which covers an area the size of Wales. The Jokkmokk Museum has a fascinating collection of Lapp artefacts while in the main street there are shops and stalls selling various Lapp handicrafts. On the outskirts is the Jokkmokk Turistcenter, a very large and rather overpowering camping site, not the place for someone wanting peace and quiet.

Occupying a more tranquil location is the Hotel Jokkmokk where I enjoyed a very reasonably priced lunch. It looks a comfortable place to stay. You continue north on road 97, and the only place along the 57 miles to *Gällivare* is Porjus where there is a large hydro-electric power station (open to the public). Before you catch sight of Gällivare (**116**) you will see the bulk of Dundret mountain (2,690 ft above sea level) and halfway up on one side is the Dundret Leisure Centre. Follow the signs on the right to reach it. There is a long low wooden hotel building – Björnfallen – with reception, restaurant, lounge, bar, shop and indoor pool while the majority of the accommodation is in wooden cabins and houses. They provide self-catering facilities but you can if you prefer take your meals in the hotel building. A new wing of the hotel, with bedrooms, has just been completed which will widen the range of accommodation available.

An enthusiastic activities staff at Dundret can organise every moment of the day for you if you wish, and riding, walking, windsurfing, fishing, golf, shooting the rapids or panning for gold are just some of the pastimes; you can hire all the necessary equipment from the centre. If, on the other hand, you want to do your own thing then no one will worry you. There are superb views from the restaurant, looking down on Gällivare and across to distant mountain ranges. You can also drive up to the top of the mountain where, on a clear day, you can see for nearly 70 miles.

Gällivare is an important iron ore mining centre and has a mining museum and some preserved Lapp buildings (complete with tame reindeer), an interesting church and a good camping site. If you have a caravan you can park it at the Dundret Centre.

DAY 7

The first part of road 98 from Gällivare to *Kiruna* (**117**) is rather uninspiring but after passing Svappavaara there are some distant views of impressive peaks. Approaching Kiruna, the other major Lapland mining centre, you see signs of the enormous iron ore workings as this is a town literally founded on iron ore.

Kirunavaara is the world's largest underground mine and below ground they not only mine the ore but have service stations, workshops, employee restaurants and computer centres. You can take a coach tour of the mine in summer. Kiruna Samegård provides a glimpse of the life and history of the Lapps.

Until the 1980's there was no highway beyond Kiruna, the railway being the only link with Norway. Since the new road – the Nordkalottvägen (**119**) – was opened throughout to Narvik in 1984 this entire area, dubbed the last wilderness of Europe, has become much more accessible. It is this road that is the climax of your journey to the north of Sweden. You enjoy spectacular views of the mountains, sharply outlined in the clear air, some of them remaining snow-capped even in midsummer. For part of the distance there is the placid and beautiful Lake Torne Träsk on the right hand side, while the vast area to the left of the road is a national park with hundreds of miles of marked trails.

Abisko Turiststation is a popular base for those walking into the wilderness while further west at *Björkliden* (turn left off the main road and go under the railway) there is the superbly sited Hotel Fjället where you can also rent self-catering cabins. The views from the hotel are dazzling – particularly from the restaurant. You can have a fishing permit (valid for 3,000 lakes) for Skr15 a day; hire a bicycle for Skr30 a day; go on a guided walking tour; have a trip on the lake for Skr110; or take a sightseeing helicopter flight for Skr150. Nearer the railway there is an older hotel – the Gammelgården – which is under the same ownership as the Fjället. Either would be suitable places to stay.

If you continue almost to the Norwegian frontier you will see the Riksgränsen Hotel (one of the Sara chain) on the left hand side. This large modern complex with 220 bedrooms offers every comfort and has an extensive restaurant, cosy bar, lounge, sauna and supermarket. A highly civilised base. Nearby is a youth hostel and a camping site.

DAY 8

While you are staying at Riksgränsen or Björkliden make a point of driving across the border to Narvik over the latest section of this magnificent new highway. There are exciting views as you gradually descend towards the E6 at the edge of the Rombakfjord (the same E6 which was mentioned right at the beginning of this itinerary and which goes through Norway all the way to Narvik). At Narvik you meet the sea once more and this is where you could add on the lengthy drive to Tromsø and the North Cape (but just check the distance before you get carried away). Riksgränsen to Narvik is an hour's drive. Stay overnight at Riksgränsen or Björkliden.

DAY 9

Return along road 98 to Kiruna for an overnight stay or continue a few miles beyond the town and turn left on the road to *Jukkasjärvi* (**118**), about five miles away. The little village ends at the painted wooden church near the small open air museum. At the Tourist Centre there is a camping site which also has cabins and across the road is the Jukkasjärvi Wärdshus which offers modest accommodation but which has a very good restaurant. It is here that you can make an exciting journey down river, shooting the rapids in a rubber boat or canoe. In winter you can go out into the white wilderness with a sledge and dog team.

At Kiruna there are two main hotels; the Ferrum with 170 rooms (Reso group) and the Kebne which has 34 rooms.

An option at this point is to take a car sleeper from Kiruna to Stockholm, spend several nights in the capital and then motor to Gothenburg.

DAY 10

It's road 98 again but instead of turning towards Gällivare you turn left to Luleå (**108**). You motor through heavily forested, gently undulating and somewhat repetitive countryside with little to break the monotony. Beyond Lansjärv watch for the Arctic Circle sign on the left hand side of the road where there is the Värdshuset Polarcirkeln. It is a café, restaurant and a gift shop and by the time this book is published there should also be some very comfortable accommodation as well. A good place for lunch because the food is of a high standard – try the röding (arctic char) which is delicious. You can also get a rather superior souvenir of crossing the Arctic Circle which includes your name on reindeer hide.

The Arctic Circle notice is a reminder as to just how far north you can travel in Sweden.

ABOVE – Looking across to Jarvsjö church with forested hills in the background.

BELOW – In the old mining town of Kopparberg the former post office is now the local tourist information centre.

ABOVE – The Ristafallet between Åre and Östersund is just one of many spectacular waterfalls to be seen.

BELOW – Tanums Gestgifveri, which dates back to 1663 and is renowned for its cuisine, is a good example of some of the delightful old inns and country hotels where you can stay or enjoy a meal.

One of the most known souvenirs are the wooden Dalarna horses. You can visit the factory at Nusnäs and watch them being made and hand painted.

Continue on the 98 all the way to Töre when you meet the E4 and turn right. Leave this road where it is signed to *Luleå* for your overnight stop. The original church town or Kyrkbyn – the Gammelstad – was founded in 1621 and is several miles from the present day Luleå, which is the largest centre in the north of Sweden. A comfortable place to stay is the SAS Globetrotter Hotel, which enjoys a central location and was opened in 1977. The restaurant is a copy of the saloon on Gustav III's galleon Amphion and there is also a bar, the Cleopatra night club, a health club and pool and 213 well-equipped bedrooms. Nearby, facing the cathedral, is the Stadshotellet which has 120 rooms. Option: At Luleå you can travel by car sleeper direct to Gothenburg, saving time and eliminating the long drive back to the west coast.

DAY 11

If you decide to spend an extra day in Luleå you should visit the Gammelstad (follow the signs to Kyrkbyn) which is dominated by the 15th century church. The little houses all around it were originally used by churchgoers coming from a long distance to attend the great church festivals and they are still used from time to time. There is an interesting open air museum at one end of the town while if you are looking for good food try Margareta's Wärdshus – snacks upstairs, more expensive meals on the ground floor. Even if you have only one night at Luleå you can spend an hour or two in this interesting old town before moving on.

You depart on the E4 to the south, bypassing Piteå which is a popular holiday centre but which I found disappointing. You continue along the main road which is something of an anti-climax after the wonderful scenery enjoyed during the previous few days. If by Skellefteå you are finding the E4 somewhat boring, bear right south of the town on to the 364 to *Burträsk*. The latter is a pleasant little village, by a lake, with an imposing church and a small open air museum (where I enjoyed delicious waffles and coffee at a very modest price). There is also a nice looking inn (Värdshus) in the village. Keep to the 364, which offers some delightful views across Lake Bygdeträsket, the road eventually swinging away to the west and then south through Botsmark. This quiet road eventually links up with the E4 on the outskirts of *Umeå* (**107**).

Umeå is your next overnight stop and this attractive town on the Ume river has numerous hotels and I found the Stora Hotellet, in the centre, to be very comfortable. Others include the Blå Aveny (modern and central), Strand, Blå Dragonen, Winn (Sara group) and Scandic (off the E4 and 1¼ miles south of the town).

DAY 12

Rejoin the inevitable E4 which rolls on through unexceptional scenery until a few miles south of Örnsköldsvik when you see the surprising outline of the Skuleberget mountain. There is a car park on the right at the foot of the mountain, plus a camping site, and you can take a chair lift to the peak cottage and look-out tower.

Between the E4 and the sea there is now what I consider to be the most beautiful area along this part of the Swedish east coast. It is called the High Coast *(Höga Kusten)* (**100**) and includes a delightful mixture of enchanting scenery: forest, lakes, meadowland, sea and rocky coastline. To gain access, leave the E4 near Ullånger, turning left, and follow the signs to Nordingrå, a pretty village where, on leaving, you turn right to Fällsvik and *Bönhamn*.

Bönhamn is a little fishing village of exceptional beauty. It is best to leave your car in the car park on the outskirts and walk down to the harbour where you can try some delicious freshly caught Baltic herring at the café overlooking the water. You can return to the main highway by following the small coastal road to Haggvik and then following signs to Gallsätter, turning left on to the E4. Continue driving south to Härnösand (**99**) which would make a suitable overnight stop if you have spent some of the day around the High Coast area. It is a pleasant town, most of it being on an island and there are several hotels including a Scandic and the Statt (one of the Sara chain).

The alternative to Härnösand is to continue to Sundsvall, then turn right on to the E75 as far as Stöde where you turn left on to the 305 which is an enjoyable scenic route, far preferable to the E4. It goes through Hassela and Friggesand, with views of the sizeable Dellen lakes, and on to Delsbo where every year there is an enormous gathering of fiddlers – the violin playing variety. Turn right on to road 84 and then left on to a secondary road to *Järvsö* (**96**) which is a sinuous and unsurfaced road but which has the compensation of providing some fine views.

At Järvsö cross the river Ljusnan and the railway and immediately afterwards turn left at the T-junction on to road 83, signed to Bollnäs. After a short distance you will see, on the left, the Krämsta Gästgård which makes an admirable place to spend the night. The hotel has been extended and modernised recently and provides comfortable rooms, those at the back looking across to the river, the church and, in the distance, the Järvsöklack, 1,279 ft above sea level (see photograph on page 110). There is a delightful restaurant with a pleasant outlook and good food. Other places to stay include the Motell Järvsö, Järvsöbaden and Solbackens Pensionat. There is also a good camping site on the western outskirts.

Järvsö itself is a pleasant little town with its large church which is on an island in the river. The old parsonage by the church tower is now a museum. On the far bank of the river is Stengårds handicraft centre where craftsmen can be seen at work – glassblowers, potters, a silversmith, a blacksmith and woodworkers. You can buy their handiwork and there is a café, while the grounds are the setting for the annual Helsinge Hambo – a folk dance contest which attracts up to 3,000 participants every year.

DAY 13

If you have stayed in Härnösand it is a case of rejoining the E4 south but if you have opted for Järvsö you leave on road 83 to Bollnäs, where you should follow the 272 signs to Kilafors. There you join the 303 which will soon link up with the E4 where you turn right. The stretch from Järvsö to the E4 is very enjoyable with some pretty views. *Gävle* (**94**) ☆, the next major centre, offers two alternatives. Option one is to head immediately for Gothenburg, while the second option is to stay with the E4 to Uppsala (**74**), Sweden's major university town, and then to continue on to Stockholm for two or more nights in the capital. From Stockholm you will once more be on the ubiquitous E4 to Jönköping where you switch to road 40 via Ulricehamn and Borås to Gothenburg.

Before describing the route for option one I would just mention that Gävle has a number of attractions including a county museum (four floors of interesting exhibits), a museum of forestry (the Silvanum) and a big railway museum, the equivalent of the National Railway Museum in York. This is on the outskirts of the town and houses a very fine collection of preserved locomotives and rolling stock, plus countless other items of interest.

You might well wish to spend the night here, in which case there are plenty of hotels to choose from including the Hotel Winn (Sara group), Triangeln, Scandic, Gävle, Aveny and the Grand Central (Reso group). Otherwise you should leave the town on the 80 which you stay with to Storvik where you switch to the 68 through Horndal, Avesta, Fagersta to Lindesberg. Then follow the signs on to the 60 to *Örebro* (**67**), your final overnight stop before Gothenburg. There is a good choice of hotels in the town or on the outskirts of Örebro including the Continental, Bergsmannen, Gullvivan, Örebro, Scandic and Grev Rosen. The latter is a modern hotel with good rooms but no restaurant (several close at hand). The centre of the town has some rather fine turn of the century buildings and is dominated by the castle, while in the park by the river are some preserved timber dwellings. For a high level view of the town take the lift to the top of 'Svampen', the huge mushroom-shaped water tower. On the outskirts near the E3 and E18 is Karlslunds Gård (**68**) where there are 90 preserved 18th and 19th century buildings set out in beautiful surroundings.

DAY 14

Drive out of Örebro on the E3 which goes through unexceptional farmland and at Götene turn right on to the 44 which bypasses Lidköping and at Vänersborg turn left on to the 45 which brings you back to the road where your journey to the Arctic Circle began. An overnight stay in Gothenburg will give you the chance to sample the city's attractions before departing on the ferry for Britain.

COUNTRY LIVING

SWEDEN HAS A NUMBER of delightful country hotels and inns. Some of them are old-established and have occupied the same buildings for hundreds of years while others are in former manor houses or mansions.

This itinerary is different from the others because it is not intended that you should visit all the country hotels I have selected. Instead you will probably prefer to pick out two or three that appeal to you or, in some cases, you can incorporate them into other itineraries.

This is very much a personal choice and all the hotels mentioned are known to me. I have arranged them in a logical geographical order, starting on the west coast and then moving north into Värmland, then east and finally south into Småland.

Each of these hotels has its own distinctive atmosphere, usually its own culinary specialities and the opportunity for relaxation with the possibility of various leisure pursuits. The accommodation varies both in style and the degree of luxury, but in every case it is comfortable.

ARILD

This small village is in the south west of Sweden and therefore it is easier to approach it via Denmark. From Harwich you drive across Denmark, over the Great Belt by ferry which links the islands of Funen and Zealand and on to the outskirts of Copenhagen. So far you have been on the E66 but now you should follow the signs on to the E4 to Helsingør. The motorway ends just short of the town and the road is then clearly marked to the ferry. The crossing is 25 minutes to Helsingborg which lies just over the Sound. Of course you can spend a night in Copenhagen, before going over to Sweden, and savour the delights of the Danish capital. Or you could stay in Helsingør which is dominated by the magnificent Kronborg Castle, the setting for Shakespeare's Hamlet.

Once ashore in Helsingborg (1) you join road 22 to Högenäs and Mölle, but before reaching the latter you turn right and after a short distance turn left down a small road to the charming little village of *Arild*. Before the road descends quite steeply to the small harbour you will see on the left the Hotel Rusthållargården. Built in 1675, it has been in the hands of the present family since the turn of the century.

Only a few years ago it was modernised, but very sympathetically, and it retains a warm and friendly atmosphere. There are 40 bedrooms and those at the front overlook the village and the sea, while just across the road is an attractive garden. The restaurant provides the right setting for the excellent food while there is a lounge and library in which to relax.

The location is restful, and the immediate area – which is more akin to Denmark than Sweden – invites some gentle exploration. Arild is on the promontory known as Kullen which is quite hilly and you get splendid views across the Kattegat to the distant shores of Denmark. Not far away there are opportunities for golf (several courses in the vicinity), tennis, sailing and fishing. *Map 1.*

SÄRÖ

Moving along the west coast to just a few miles south of Gothenburg there is the town of Kungsbacka. Leave the E4 here, go through the town and follow the signs to Särö (**14**). The road twists and turns until it comes out by the sea, where you will find, perched up above the rocky coastline, the Säröhus Hotel.

This is a traditional style wooden hotel, with magnificent views out to sea. The bedrooms are quite simple and on the ground floor is the delightful Oscar II's dining room, while there are several other rooms, together with a small bar and lounge. The food is excellent and the atmosphere friendly. The hotel has 42 bedrooms, its own tennis court and a sauna.

Särö became fashionable as a seaside resort in the middle of the 19th century, due in no small measure to royal patronage as it was popular with both King Oscar II and the tennis-playing Gustav V (the tennis courts on which he played are still in use today). In the past it was linked by a little narrow-gauge railway from Gothenburg but this has disappeared, except for the former station building at Särö which is now a restaurant.

It is a quiet place, with its rocky coast and scattering of islets while the shore is backed by woods and low hills. You can walk along the Strandpromenaden through the Särö Västerskog, where you will find huge old oak trees. The buildings around have a turn of the century look to them, with their ornamental carved woodwork around the verandas and balconies.

In summer you can go on a seal safari, being taken out in a launch to view the large colonies of seals. There are other places to visit in the area: the town of Kungsbacka; the fishing harbour at Lerkil; Tjolöholm with its somewhat surprising Tudor-style castle (**13**) which was built about 1900; and Äskhult, which is a preserved hamlet which gives a good idea of how a small farming community lived in the 18th century (**15**). There are several small bathing beaches in the vicinity, plus a golf course (you pass it on the way from Kungsbacka) while at Särö itself you can hire rowing, sailing and motor boats. Should you tire of the seaside life then you are not far away from the big city of Gothenburg. *Map 1.*

TANUMSHEDE

This little town lies just off the E6 about 20 miles south of Strömstad and on its outskirts you will see, set back from the road, Tanums Gestgifveri. This old-established inn, with its timbers painted in the traditional biscuit colour, opened its doors in 1663. It is very widely known and has an outstanding reputation for its fine cuisine which is very much the province of the proprietor and chef, Mr Steiner

Öster, ably assisted by his wife Regine.

There are several charming little dining rooms, all with the right ambience, where you are served by equally charming young ladies. Fish is the speciality – shellfish, salmon, sole, halibut, brill – while you can start your meal with Smögen herring, Swedish red roe or fish paté. Highly recommended is the 'Fish Pot' which is delicious.

The accommodation is in a separate, but similar style, building and there are 25 rooms. The bedrooms are very tasteful and there are some more expensive de-luxe rooms – the 'Kings Suite' and the 'Residenset' – which allow you to indulge in delusions of grandeur. There is a sauna and plunge pool.

At nearby *Tanum* (**20**) and in the immediate area there are the amazing Bronze Age rock carvings which give the news in pictures – as it was 3,000 years ago. Call at the Tanum Rock Carving Institute which will show you where they are. The sea is not far away – less than five miles – at Grebbestad, while the coast is dotted with picturesque little fishing villages. You can find plenty of places to bathe or to try your hand at sea fishing. Nearest golf course is at Fjällbacka. Longer excursions: drive up the E6 to Norway for the day, or go and see the remarkable aqueduct on the Dalsland canal at Håverud (**22**). *Maps 1 and 2.*

SUNNE

Leave Gothenburg on road 45 and as you near the northern end of Lake Vänern go left at Grums on road 234 to Sunne, continue north beyond the town on this road and after about two miles you will find, on the right hand side, *Länsmansgården*. It lies at the end of a long drive and is a former manor house. In the main building are the restaurant and lounges which are most attractive while some of the 30 bedrooms are in a separate building. All are nicely decorated and furnished. The large garden, at the rear of the hotel, goes down to Fryken lake where there is a private beach and rowing boats and canoes. There is also free fishing in the lake. There is a golf course just south of Sunne.

I didn't have the opportunity of eating at Länsmansgården, but I understand that the cuisine is excellent.

One of Sweden's most famous writers, Selma Lagerlöf, lived in this area and you can visit her home, now preserved as it was when she was alive, at Mårbacka (**27**). Also in this area is some splendid scenery, not to mention the beautiful Rottneros Park (**26**) with its gardens and statues. *Maps 2 and 3.*

UDDEHOLM

Through the heart of Värmland, following the course of the gently flowing Klarälven river is the Pilgrims Way. The pilgrims crossed Lake Vänern then trudged north west to Norway to visit the grave of Olav the Holy in Trondheim. Both their route and the river skirted

Lake Råda.

Latter day pilgrims, in search of comfort and good food, should motor to *Uddeholm* on the north bank of Lake Råda where they will find Uddeholms Brukshotel. You take road 45 to Karlstad, then road 63, bearing left on the 240 which takes you to the little town of Uddeholm. The hotel lies back from the road, in spacious grounds and the lawns at the rear stretch down to the lake. At one time the hotel buildings were owned by a steelworks and used as living quarters for the staff. It is now a most enjoyable place to stay, and don't be put off by the word 'steelworks' because today it's quiet and peaceful with no sign of industry.

The main building (like the others) is painted in the traditional biscuit colour and houses the restaurant and lounges and some conference rooms. The bedrooms are in three separate buildings (all overlooking the lake) and these have been attractively decorated and furnished and each building also has its own lounge. There is a total of 60 beds.

The hotel has something of a reputation for the quality of its food and this is due to the enterprise of its personable German chef, Hans Mallwitz. They also have a very good cellar and their own house 'snaps' which is appropriately called 'steel and iron'.

The hotel has hard tennis courts while you can go windsurfing or water skiing on the lake. You can rent a canoe or rowing boat or

119

go fishing for perch, pike or eel. Conveniently close is a good 18-hole golf course while less than a mile away is the Uddeholm Riding School.

To work up an appetite or take off a little weight there is an exercise room and sauna plus billiards and table tennis.

You can explore the surrounding area with its splendid scenery, motoring along good roads with very little traffic. *Maps 2 and 3.*

FILIPSTAD

If instead of taking road 234 to Uddeholm you continue along the 63 you will soon come to Filipstad. In the centre turn right on to the 64 to Mariestad and less than a mile away you will see a small road on the left to *Hennickehammar*. A mile and a quarter along this unsurfaced road (don't let the lack of asphalt put you off) you will come to Hennickehammars Herrgård.

Several centuries ago this part of Värmland was the heart of the important iron working industry. Today the only traces of all this industrial activity are to be found in museums and in preserved smelters. Hennickehammar was the manor house home of one of the iron masters. Today it is a very inviting country hotel, sited in beautiful surroundings beside Lake Hemtjärn. The present owners, Mr and Mrs Bjorn Sandefelt have created an hotel where you feel more like a welcome house guest than merely a room number.

The kitchen achieves a high standard in the preparation and presentation of the meals which are served in the elegant dining room. The lounges are a positive invitation to sink into an easy chair and relax. The majority of the 62 bedrooms are furnished in an individual style and in keeping with the building.

You can fish (rods provided) in the lake, row a boat, try windsurfing, play tennis on the hotel's court or wander around the extensive grounds. There are plenty of marked trails in the area suitable for walking or jogging and on your return you can always have a sauna. You can ride at a nearby school and nine miles away, at Saxå, is a nine-hole golf course.

The surrounding area provides plenty of scenic beauty as well as reasons for the occasional excursion – such as a visit to Långban Herrgård (**32**), the birthplace of inventor John Ericsson and his engineer brother Nils. *Maps 2 and 3.*

GRYTHYTTAN

The country hotel trail continues along road 63 beyond Filipstad to Hammarn where you turn right on to road 244 and after about five miles you reach *Grythyttan*. Turn right and enter the little town and near the old market place you will see on the left Grythyttan Gästgivaregård.

This inn was built on the orders of Queen Christina in 1640 at the time a road was constructed. The town was the centre of the iron smelting industry and at its peak it must have been a busy, bustling place. When the iron making came to an end Grythyttan became a backwater and even the inn was closed in 1878.

Today it is open again and flourishing while the little town is in something of a time warp with much of it unchanged from the busier days of long ago. The inn has achieved an international reputation thanks to the enterprise of its proprietor, Carl Jan Granqvist. He has proved that if you offer the best in food, drink, comfort and culture, people will beat a path to your door – even if it is in some quiet corner of Bergslagen (**80**).

Apart from the main building, all the surrounding houses – on both sides of the road – have gradually been acquired for additional accommodation. So you may find that your bedroom is in the Coppersmith's Cottage or Gustaf Per's Cottage. Altogether there are 120 beds. The main building includes three tastefully decorated dining rooms and several lounges, furnished with antiques, including the splendid Karl Johan lounge. This is also the scene of cultural entertainments from time to time.

The inn is renowned for attracting the top people as its guests so you never know who may be sitting at an adjoining table while you savour some delightful gastronomic experience. You can also enjoy some very fine wine from Grythyttan's extensive cellar.

Granqvist is a former antique dealer and art historian and his expertise in these areas is apparent as you enjoy the atmosphere of this unusual hostelry.

In the surrounding area you can fish, walk, ride, cycle, play golf or tennis or try your hand at canoeing. *Maps 2 and 3.*

SVARTÅ

Still within the Bergslagen area (**80**) is Svartå Herrgård which is on road 205 between Degerfors and Laxå. This well-proportioned Gustavian mansion was built for the Marshal of the Court Carl Falker in 1775 – 1782. For many years the house belonged to Svartå Bruk, another company involved in iron founding, much later becoming an hotel. Now Marianne and Nils Frantzen, assisted by various members of their family, run Svartå Herrgård, creating an easy-going atmosphere, making it more like a country house.

You dine in the charming 'blue dining room', the excellent fare matching the surroundings while your after dinner coffee is taken in the grand salon with its period furnishings. There are 65 beds and the bedrooms are in the main buildings and the adjoining single storey wings.

The spacious grounds extend to Lake Lillbjörken where you can bathe, go for a row or fish. Indoors you can play billiards or table tennis. *Maps 2 and 3.*

KARLSBORG

On the west coast of Lake Vättern on road 49, which runs from

Askersund to Skara, lies the town of *Karlsborg* notable for its vast fortress. On the northern edge of the town road 49 crosses the Göta Canal (**132**) and right at the point where this happens is the Kanalhotellet. It was built in 1894 by Johan and Anna Axelsson and today the third generation of the family, Ruth and Petter Axelsson are in charge.

This is no luxury establishment, but a family hotel in the best sense of the word. The dining room overlooks the canal, and you can watch people messing about in boats while enjoying good food – try the röding (arctic char) which is excellent. The 25 bedrooms include some in a single storey motel-style building.

This is an hotel to use more as a base when exploring the area between lakes Vättern and Vänern. Of course you can idle away your time by watching the boats on the canal as they make their way to and from Lake Vättern, or you can take a trip on the canal. But you should see the fortress (**37** ☆) which took 90 years to build and was outdated by the time it was finished. The main building is 2,224 ft long, while the ramparts are three miles long. Worth looking at is the garrison church and the military museum. There is also some very pleasant scenery in the vicinity. *Map 2.*

HOK

At the southern tip of Vättern is Jönköping and if you leave the town on the E4 and after about 18 miles turn left on to road 36 you will, just before you reach the village of Hok, see Hook Manor, which is on the left hand side at the end of a long driveway. The present house was built in the 18th century and the adjoining farm buildings and barns have been skilfully converted into modern conference facilities. It should be said at the outset that Hook Manor thrives on conference business and you are very likely to find keen executives forming a major part of the guest list.

The main building includes several beautiful salons furnished in period style while the new restaurant, which overlooks the lake, is quite stunning with its modern, but tasteful, decorative scheme. There is also a cosy bar.

Apart from bedrooms in the manor house there are others in the surrounding buildings, each of which has been given a distinctive name, such as Cavalier's Wing or Rose Wing. Rooms are well furnished, and there is also a luxury suite which features a bubble pool for two and a private sitting room.

There are enough activities to keep you occupied within the grounds of the hotel. They include golf (the hotel has its own course), badminton, fishing, tennis, windsurfing and swimming in the outdoor heated salt-water pool. You can also borrow a canoe or rowing boat, jog around the exercise track or work out in the exercise room. There are plenty of places to visit in the immediate area. *Map 1.*

TOFTAHOLM

Travelling south on the E4, you begin to parallel Lake Vidöstern after you have passed Värnamo. Towards the end of the lake between Tånnö and Dörarp there lies, some distance back from the road, Toftaholm Herrgårdshotell which is several hundred years old. The main building is flanked by two detached wings while the extensive grounds stretch to the lake some 25 yards away. You can paddle a canoe, go windsurfing or try your hand at fishing. There is also a castle ruin on a small island in the lake which you can reach by footbridge.

This is essentially a quiet spot where you can enjoy good food in the pleasant dining room or relax in the attractive lounge. There are 32 comfortable rooms. Toftaholm is also said to possess a friendly ghost. *Map 1.*

DELIGHTFUL DALARNA AND VÄRMLAND

THE INVITING BUT CONTRASTING counties of Dalarna and Värmland are featured in this itinerary. Before you reach either of these provinces there are opportunities of seeing places of interest along the way.

Starting from Gothenburg there is, on the first day, the possibility of visiting Läckö Castle on Lake Vänern before staying at either Hjo or Karlsborg on the shores of Lake Vättern. The next day you can see a little more of this 'between the lakes' region before continuing to Örebro. Here you could add on an excursion to Stockholm if time permits. Otherwise you move on to Tällberg, which enjoys a beautiful position on Lake Siljan. You see, on the way, the 'copper town' of Falun and the delightful little lakeside resort of Leksand.

You are now in the heart of Dalarna, the folklore county of Sweden, and a deservedly popular holiday area. You can either spend two nights at Tällberg, or one night here and one night in Mora. There is plenty to occupy your time in this area, and if you can I would suggest you extend your stay by at least another night.

After leaving Lake Siljan you drive into the tranquil and delightful county of Värmland with its lovely Klarälven valley, heading for either Uddeholm or N. Råda. Your journey of exploration continues into the charming Fryken lake district to Sunne where you stay for two nights.

Your journey continues to Arvika for an overnight stay before driving back to Gothenburg for your final night before returning to the UK.

The minimum number of nights is nine, but if you want to see Stockholm or spend more time in Dalarna or Värmland then you need to extend your stay to 11 or 12 nights. *Maps 2, 3 and 4.*

DAY 1

Leave Gothenburg on the E3 to Alingsås, a peaceful little country town. If you want a diversion follow the signs on to the secondary road to Anten, where there is a preserved railway (**35**) ☆ which has a pretty lakeside route to Gräfsnäs terminating by a park with castle ruins. If you drive to Gräfsnäs you should continue to Sollebrun and turn right on the 42 (signed to Borås) and you will rejoin the E3 on the approach to Vårgårda (turn left).

At Vara look for the left turn which takes you on to road 187. It cuts through unexciting farmland until you reach the outskirts of Lidköping (**44**) where you should follow the signs to *Läckö*. Now the scenery is much prettier and your journey's end is the magnificent Läckö Castle (**36**) ☆ which has a wonderful position at the very tip of the Kållandsö peninsula. Return the same way to Lidköping and then take road 44 to begin with before turning right on to the Skara road. On the approach to Skara (**40**) follow the signs to Skövde. Five miles from Skara, on the left, is the turn to Skara Sommarland (**39**) ☆ – a marvellous place for children, but they will need more than an hour or two to even see, let alone try, all the attractions.

You will get some fine views as you approach Skövde where you should take either the 194 to *Hjo* or 49 to *Karlsborg*. These are your alternative overnight stops. Hjo (**38**) is a charming lakeside resort, and in a central position is the modern and comfortable Hotel Bellevue. Karlsborg (**37**) ☆ is a small town dominated by the massive fortress and on its outskirts the Göta Canal enters Lake Vättern and this is also where you will find the unpretentious but friendly Kanalhotellet (see 'Country Living' for details). If you can spare two nights at whichever centre you choose, you could explore more of this very enjoyable region.

DAY 2

If you have stayed at Hjo, take road 195 to Karlsborg. From the latter your route is on road 49 to Askersund, at the northern end of Lake Vättern; here you switch to road 50 which joins the E3 to *Örebro*. This is your next overnight stop and as the mileage from Hjo or Karlsborg is modest you have the option of spending more time 'between the lakes' or exploring some of the places of interest in and around Örebro (**67**). In the centre of the town is the castle which, although very traditional in appearance, only dates from the end of the 19th century. At one end of the town park, which is skirted on one side by the river, is Wadköping, a collection of old wooden dwellings where you can spend a quiet hour or so looking round or, alternatively, go to Karlslunds Gård (**68**) just outside the town. This has a fine collection of old buildings from the 18th and 19th centuries ranging from a cow shed to a tavern.

It is from Örebro that you can conveniently add on an excursion to Stockholm for one or two nights. You can either take the E18 (north of Lake Mälaren) or the E3 (south of the lake). I would opt for the latter as it lets you make a quick detour to Mariefred (**71**) ☆ and Gripsholm Castle (**72**).

DAY 3

Take road 60 from Örebro and later turn left on the 244 to *Nora* (**78**), a pastoral drive through undulating farmland. Nora is a small, quiet town in the heart of the old mining area. Like so many Swedish towns it is on a lake, and down near the water you can enjoy coffee and cakes in a beautifully preserved wooden dining car that once belonged to the Nora Bergslagens Railway. When I called at the diner I was served by the prettiest of waitresses who had spent some time as an au pair in Tooting which must have been something of a contrast to Nora.

From time to time you can ride a preserved steam train from here, while just outside the town at Pershyttan (**79**) there are guided tours of a mine and smelting house which has the largest water-wheel in Sweden in working order.

The mining industry is a thing of the past and what remains

today is a peaceful landscape with frequent forests and lakes and numerous attractive little roads. You take one of these secondary roads from Nora to Storå which parallels Lake Norasjö before you cross the river to travel along the shores of Lake Fåsjön to Siggebohyttan. Here you can turn right on a minor unsurfaced road which climbs over a ridge of hills and comes out on road 60 where you turn left and continue through Fanthyttan and Storå. Watch for the sign to Löa, a nice little village with a preserved smelter which is now a museum.

The 60 brings you through *Kopparberg* (**76**), which is worth a short stop, and on through Grangesberg (**86**) ☆ to Ludvika (**87**) ☆ where there is an interesting mining museum. At Borlänge (**84**) stay with road 60 to *Falun* (**85**), the famous 'copper town' which is the oldest known industrial town and was called 'Sweden's treasure chest'. As you come into the town the old mine and the Stora Kopparberg Museum – both worth seeing – are on the left. Shortly after resuming your journey turn left on to road 293 to Leksand (**88**). North east of Falun is Sundborn, where there is the home and studio of artist Carl Larsson – worth a detour if you have the time. You are now on the edge of the beautiful area surrounding Lake Siljan.

After a pause at Leksand (see the open air museum and the church) you continue on the minor road alongside the lake through Hjortnas with its fascinating museum of miniature metal figures (**89**) ☆ to *Tällberg*.

Tällberg is a beautiful village on a hillside stretching down to the lake and it is also where a number of craftsmen have their workshops or studios. Here you stay for two nights and there are numerous hotels to choose from including the Dalecarlia (60 rooms), Green Hotel (89 rooms – high above the lake), Klockargården (an hotel with a handicrafts shop and which is close to the lake), Siljansgården (on the lake shore, 23 rooms) and Åkerblads (a family hotel with 50 rooms which is also near the lake).

DAY 4

There is a considerable choice for you on your free day in the heart of Dalarna but one obvious excursion is to drive around Lake Siljan. From Tällberg you come first to *Rättvik*, with its Gammelgård (**90**), an open air museum with a fine collection of costumes, Dalecarlian paintings and furnishings. Beside the old church are the unusual 16th - 17th century church stables where the horses were tied up during the services. There is also a landing stage for the church boats – these brought the faithful to services because roads were almost non-existent.

Beyond Rättvik at the village of Fudal, turn left to Nusnäs (**91**) ☆ and then watch for the right turn signed to *Dalahäst tillverkning*. This is where the famous brightly painted wooden Dalecarlian horses are made. After pausing to watch these horses being manufactured and expertly hand-painted (and possibly buying one or two for souvenirs) you continue until you rejoin the main road near *Mora* (**92**). The latter is the biggest town on the lake and a popular holiday centre. This could be an alternative for your stay in this area. There is the very comfortable and central Mora Hotel which has 91 rooms and an excellent restaurant. There is also the Hotel Ljustret (one of the Reso group) in Mora Parken where there is also a youth hostel and camping site, and on the edge of the town is the Scandic Hotel.

Instead of keeping to the main road beyond Mora you can drive across to the island of Sollerön which is a peaceful, rural spot referred to as the 'eye of the sun in Lake Siljan'. This is because it claims to have the warmest and sunniest climate in the Siljan district. There are over 100 Viking graves on Sollerön. Return, via a causeway, to the mainland where you can then drive up the Gesunda mountain (**93**) ☆ from the top of which (1,689 ft above sea level) you will get a fine view of the lake. Part way up is Tomteland or Santaworld (**93**) ☆ where children can visit Santa's workshop and also such attractions as the Snow Queen's Palace and Sleigh House. Personally I have doubts about this commercial exploitation of poor old Father Christmas.

The road round the southern end of the lake is quite rural until you are back to Leksand. Apart from Lake Siljan you can also drive round Lake Orsa which lies to the north of Mora. Leave the town on road 295 then turn right on the secondary road to Bonås and Våmhus, where you turn right to Hansjö and Orsa. When you reach road 81 turn right and this will bring you back to Mora. A modest but enjoyable circuit with nothing of special note, except that near Orsa on the left is Grönklint where there is a bear park.

Anders Zorn, one of Sweden's most famous painters, lived and worked in Mora and you can see his home, and also a museum containing examples of his work. On the outskirts of the town is the extensive Forestry Museum (forests cover seven tenths of Dalarna) which is worth a visit. Another alternative is to go for a cruise on the lake on the 1876 vintage steamer 'Gustaf Wasa'. If you motor only about 15 miles north of Mora you are among the mountains of north Dalarna in the sparsely inhabited but beautiful Älvdalen district – which is yet another alternative for you.

DAY 5

From Mora, drive out on road 242 and later turn right on to the 234 through Öje and Malung to N. Ny where you come to road 62. Turn left and you are on a road which follows the slow-moving and winding course of the Klarälven river through splendid Värmland scenery: forests, hills and meadows (see the photograph on page 35).

At *Eksharad* (**29**) look at the interesting church with its wrought iron crosses in place of headstones in the graveyard. Continue through Edebäck where you bear left on the 246 towards Hagfors but after only a mile down this road you will come to Uddeholm. On the right, by the lake, is the welcoming Uddeholms Brukshotell (see 'Country Living' for more details). This makes an enjoyable overnight base, but an alternative would be to continue on the 62, instead of turning on to the 246, to N. Råda where there is Björns Wärdshus (30 rooms). There is also a good camping site which has a sandy beach at the lakeside.

If you have time for a further excursion stay on the 62 through Munkfors (where there is Sweden's first open-hearth iron works which is now a museum) to *Ransäter* (**21**) ☆. Here you will be able to wander round the interesting Hembygsgården or homestead museum. It has a collection of old buildings, some of which are museums devoted to mining, forestry, agriculture and rural life in bygone days. There is also a manor house, an inn (in use) and a tilt hammer driven by a waterwheel which was originally used for forging iron. Each year a local folk play is performed in the open air theatre. Adjoining the museum are some self-catering cabins, in traditional style, by the lake.

After leaving Ransäter turn left to Olsäter where you take another left turn on to a minor unsurfaced road which has plenty of ups and downs until you reach a T-junction (turn left); this road joins the 240 at Älvsbacka where you make another left turn. After passing Sunnemo (notable wooden church) you will come to Uddeholm or alternatively you can return to N. Råda, depending on where you are staying.

DAY 6

Return on road 62 to Eksharad where you turn left, by the church, on to a secondary road which cuts across thinly inhabited and undulating country towards Torsby. Follow the signs which bring you to the outskirts of this little town at the northern end of the Fryken lakes. There is nothing of particular note here but there is a pleasant hotel, Torsby Herrgård, which is in park-like surroundings.

Leave Torsby on road 234, which parallels Övre Fryken lake, and half-way along its length look for a right turn to Tossebergsklätten (**28**). The road climbs with the aid of some hairpin bends up to the summit where there are glorious views over the lake and surrounding countryside. There is a restaurant at the top.

At the end of Övre Fryken is the town of *Sunne* which is where you should stay for two nights. There is a variety of hotel accommodation and near the town, on the left, is the Länsmansgården which would make a comfortable choice (see 'Country Living' for additional details). In Sunne itself is the Hotel Gästis (37 rooms) and on the southern side of the town is the large, modern and impressive Hotel Selma Lagerlöf. It has 156 air-conditioned rooms and a stunning restaurant with a mouth-watering lunch-time smörgåsbord. Quite expensive, so if you are looking for budget accommodation drive down to Rottneros where there is a small self-catering development with an adjoining cafeteria.

DAY 7

Sunne, between the 50-mile long Fryken lakes, is in the heart of a very pleasant area of Värmland. About five miles from the town at *Mårbacka* (**27**) is the birthplace and home of one of Sweden's greatest literary figures, Selma Lagerlöf (after whom the hotel is named). Selma Lagerlöf, born in 1858, was the first woman to receive the Noble Prize for literature. The present house at Mårbacka was where she lived from 1923 and the interior is exactly as it was when she died in 1940. Among her best known works were 'The Saga of Gösta Berling' and 'The Adventures of Nils Holgersson'.

You should also see Rottneros Park (**26**) which is roughly three miles south of Sunne on road 234. The extensive park includes 100 sculptures by famous Scandinavian and European artists, plus gardens and an arboretum – a superb location with an elegant restaurant and coffee shop.

If you missed out on the visit to Ransäter earlier in the itinerary you can easily get there from Sunne, using road 241 to Munkfors. You can also make a round trip by driving south on the 62 beyond Ransäter and Forshaga until you meet road 61 when you go right and then, on reaching the southern tip of Lake Nedre Fryken, turn right on the secondary road which will take you along the eastern side of the lake through Ö. Ämtervik (where Selma Lagerlöf is buried) to Sunne.

DAY 8

From Sunne go south on the 234 to V. Ämtervik and turn right on the secondary road to Finnebäck. This road climbs up to a high point – Fryksdalshöjden – where you can park and enjoy the view over the lake (a wooden observation tower provides some additional height).

At Finnebäck, turn right on the 61 and then left near Brunskog church on to a minor road to Edane. Down by the lake at Brunskog **(25)** is a collection of old buildings which form Gammelvala ('the old world') and where for a brief period in summer all the local crafts and skills are performed.

When you get to Edane turn right and then left on to a twisting unsurfaced little road to Högerud where you go left, and this will bring you to the 175 where it is left again and after a short distance you will see a sign on the right to *Klässbol*. Make the turn and then look for the Linnevaveri **(24)** which is a small traditional linen weaving mill which has been in the hands of the same family for three generations. They produce some very fine linen designs and you can see round the factory and also visit the shop. The mill provides all the table linen for the Swedish diplomatic corps.

Leave Klässbol and turn left on the 175 for the 13 miles to *Arvika*, which is in the centre of the Jösse district and enjoys a delightful position by a lake. This is your last night stop in Värmland and I can strongly recommend the Hotel Oscar Statt which is a traditional looking building in the main shopping street. The interior has been tastefully redecorated and modernised throughout and there are 43 bedrooms and a first class restaurant. There is a parking area at the back of the hotel. Other hotels are the Bristol (38 rooms) and the Arkaden (19 rooms, bed and breakfast only).

If you have time to spare you could easily spend another night at Arvika and then explore this quiet but enjoyable area. You can also go on the lake or go walking in the vast Glaskogen area where there are over 150 miles of marked trails. You can camp there or stay in a wooden cabin. The region is rich in wild life – both animals and birds.

DAY 9

Leave Arvika on road 174, which curves across 25 miles of undulating countryside to Vännaka where you turn left on the 172 to Årjäng. Here you cross the E18 and stay on the 172 which is an enjoyable road through Gustavsfors and Bengtsfors and on through Billingfors (a paper-making town). Just beyond Billingfors you can turn left around the end of Lake Laxsjön to Baldersnäs **(23)** where a peaceful estate occupies a promontory jutting out into the lake. The history of the estate has been closely bound up with the Dalslands Ironworks and the main house is in the style of an Italian villa while the spacious grounds include 240 species of trees. The grounds are open to the public and there is also a car museum.

After this little excursion return to the 172 and continue

through Bäckefors and on through rural scenery all the way to the outskirts of Uddevalla where you join the E6 for the final leg of your journey to Gothenburg. Overnight in Sweden's second largest city before returning to the UK.

STOCKHOLM

BIRGER JARL, one of Sweden's great historic figures, got it right when in the 13th century he picked a site to build a fort. He may have been thinking purely of defence but the present day outcome of his decision is Stockholm, a capital city of considerable beauty which enjoys a superb location. Built on 14 islands, it has to the east a complex archipelago of 22,000 islands and skerries stretching over 50 miles out into the Baltic. To the west there is Lake Mälaren which, with its own quota of islands, extends for some 80 miles.

The core of the city is relatively compact and walkable (but by no means flat), while in total it covers a considerable area. Fortunately it has well-developed urban and suburban transport networks, and when you are exploring an unfamiliar city, using the bus and underground system can make better sense than using the car.

Driving in Stockholm is not unduly difficult providing you know where you are going or are one of those drivers who are inherently street-wise when it comes to inner city navigation. There are some complex junctions, the worst probably being Slussen, a circular multi-level affair which was originally designed when Sweden drove on the left.

The choice of public transport or your car brings me neatly to one of the capital's best tourist attractions – the Stockholm Card. This piece of plastic is available with four periods of validity and the current cost is: 24 hours Skr64, 48 hours Skr108, 72 hours Skr162 and 96 hours Skr216. Children aged six and under 18 are half price.

First of all the card is valid for unlimited travel by bus, underground and on the trains of the city and county local transit system (SL). The underground, the T-Bana, has three basic lines with several additional branches and 94 stations and is highly efficient. The buses of the Stockholm Transit Authority (SL) also provide a well developed network of services which extend as far as Norrtälje in the north and Nynäshamn in the south. SL buses serve a number of the islands in the archipelago, reaching their destinations via local ferries.

The SL local trains stretch out some lengthy tentacles, for example to the seaside town of Saltsjöbaden and to Kungsängen and Märsta in the north-west and Nynäshamn and Gnesta in the south-east and south-west.

The Stockholm Card includes free sightseeing trips by coach or boat and you also get a reduction on the steamers from Stadshusbron to Drottningholm. Finally it gives you free admission to over 50 museums and attractions all over the city.

You get a compact 94-page pocket guide to where it can be used, complete with maps, and each place of interest is briefly described with opening hours, how to reach it by public transport and also what facilities are available (such as parking, refreshments, etc).

I have left to last one other splendid advantage of the card which is particularly significant to readers of this book: free parking. All tourists who buy a Stockholm Card can have a parking voucher which is valid for the same period as the card. It can be used in all car parks or parking spaces with meters which are controlled by the City of Stockholm or Stockholms Stads Parkeringsbolag AB. It is not valid for use in privately-controlled open air or multi-storey car parks.

The card can be bought at the Tourist Centre in Sweden House, Kungsträdgården (opposite the NK department store); the accommodation booking centre, Hotellcentralen, at the Central railway station; the tourist office at the City Hall; The Kaknäs TV tower; the SL Centre, Sergels Torg; and at Pressbyrån newspaper kiosks. The Tourist Centre can, of course, provide you with all the information you might need on the city and its environs. They have a useful little guide called 'What to see and do in and around Stockholm', which I can recommend. There are also two maps which are worth buying: the Official Tourist Map of Stockholm, with street index (Skr5), and Stockholm County Map (Skr16). For guidance on parking there is a free map available pinpointing car parks and also one-way and pedestrianised streets – absolutely vital information.

One area where it is best to leave the car behind is the Old Town or Gamla Stan. This is the original Stockholm, packed on to a small island with narrow streets and retaining much of its original character. It is a lively place with lots of antique and bric-à-brac shops and boutiques plus plenty of interesting restaurants in all price ranges – some with entertainment. At one end of the island is the imposing bulk of the Royal Palace where you can watch the changing of the guard (noon Mondays to Saturdays and 1.00 p.m. Sundays). You can spend hours in the Palace, visiting the apartments, the treasury, the armoury, the Hall of State, the Palace Church, the Palace Museum and the Museum of Antiquities.

On the island is Stockholm Cathedral – the *Storkyrkan* – with its remarkable wooden sculpture of St. George and the Dragon from 1489. It is in this Cathedral that Swedish royalty are christened, crowned and married while many of them are buried at the nearby *Riddarholmskyrkan*. Also in the Gamla Stan is the *Tyska Kyrkan*, the German church of St. Gertrud, and the *Riddarhuset*, the House of Nobles, while on the adjoining little island of Helgeandsholmen are the Houses of Parliament.

Stockholm is particularly rich in museums with over 50 of them covering a wealth of fascinating subjects. Choose from a range as diverse as the Museum of Dance and the Tobacco Museum or the Museum of Architecture and the Toy Museum.

One museum that should not be missed is that devoted to the warship Wasa. This ill-fated man-of-war capsized in Stockholm harbour on its maiden voyage in 1628. Recovered in 1961, the vessel has been painstakingly restored, a most remarkable achievement.

The Wasa Museum is on *Djurgården*, an extensive park-like area which includes Skansen, the interesting open air folk museum with buildings from many different parts of Sweden. It is on a hilly site, but at the top you can catch your breath and have some refreshment at the restaurant Solliden and enjoy the views. Other attractions on Djurgården include the zoo and Gröna Lund Tivoli, complete with its full quota of stomach-churning rides and all kinds of side-shows.

The 17th century Royal Palace of Drottningholm is on the island of Lovön and is bridge-connected, but a pleasant way to get there is by steamer. The Palace was designed as a smaller version of Versailles and although it is the permanent home of the Swedish Royal Family, part of the magnificent interior can be seen. In the extensive grounds is the Court Theatre, claimed to be the oldest theatre in the world still using its original scenery and stage machinery. Performances are regularly held there. An unlikely sight at the end of the Palace Park is the Chinese Pavilion.

Stockholm's best known landmark is the Town Hall which was built between 1911 and 1923. The interior includes the fabulous Golden and Blue Halls while you can go to the top of the tower for some good views. An even better view of Stockholm can be obtained from the top of the Kaknäs TV tower which is 508 ft high.

Another city view is obtainable from the *Katarina hissen*, across on Södermalm. It is a vertical lift with a restaurant at the top. Södermalm – which was the birthplace of Greta Garbo – also has some old streets with wooden buildings which contrast sharply with the city's modern architecture.

On the island of Lidingö is *Millesgården*, a spectacular museum of fountains and sculptures by the artist, Carl Milles.

Seeing the city and its surroundings from one of the numerous sightseeing boats is both appropriate and relaxing and there are many different examples to choose from. An evening cruise to the archipelago, with dinner on board the steamer, is a wonderful way to end the day. There are also the scheduled services of the Vaxholm Steamship Co., which provide connections to a whole host of destinations. Vaxholm itself is a delightful little waterfront town with a fortress museum.

In the surrounding area – and easily accessible – are many other places of interest: Norrtälje, with its Museum of Humour; Gustavsberg, with its porcelain factory which has been established for 150 years; Gripsholm Castle at Mariefred which can be reached by steamer; and Skokloster, a 17th century mansion with superb interiors and a vintage car museum.

Stockholm offers plenty of entertainment: theatre, opera, ballet, musical shows, nightclubs, discos and jazz clubs. To sustain you there are over 500 restaurants, from fast food cafeterias to expensive and world-renowned restaurants like the Operakällaren with its grand fin-de-siècle decor. There are many speciality restaurants from Czech to Chinese, while others offer food and entertainment, such as Maxim or Metropol. If you want to dance to big band sounds visit Aladdin with its huge dance floor and slightly oriental decor. For jazz try Stampen in the heart of the old town while an old-established and traditional centre for food and entertainment is Berns Salonger.

Two restaurants I liked in the Gamla Stan were Cattelin (French with a Swedish touch) and Aurora (candlelit atmosphere under vaulted stone arches) but I could just as well have listed a dozen others. In the city centre I enjoyed both the food and ambience of Riché which also includes the adjoining Teatergrillen. Both offer quiet, unobtrusive service.

For lunch you can choose from an enormous range of possibilities, from a sandwich in a cafeteria to the sumptuous smörgåsbord at the top class Grand Hotel. Most restaurants, however, offer very good value fixed-price menus – I had an excellent lunch, costing Skr35 at the Daily News café which overlooks the Kungsträdgården. There has also been something of a revival recently among the traditional type of café for coffee and light refreshments. If you enjoy looking at food pay a visit to Saluhallen, in Östermalmstorg, a large indoor market offering fish, meat, game, poultry, cheese, fruit and vegetables. There are lots of cafés in the market if you are suddenly assailed by pangs of hunger.

If you want to shop (or window shop) for things other than food, then Stockholm will meet your requirements in fine style. There is temptation in plenty, but if you want to find cheaper prices try the shops on Södermalm.

Stockholm has a good range of accommodation with something like 130 hotels to choose from. They start at the top, with such establishments as the Grand or Sheraton Stockholm, and run the whole way down the scale to simple bed and breakfast pensions. In the upper echelon I rate the Diplomat highly with its waterfront position on Strandvägen. It is quiet and comfortable and not too large (132 rooms) and has a unique Tea House and a cosy bar. The Park Hotel is another enjoyable base for the visitor. It is slightly off centre, by the Humlegården, and has 205 bedrooms.

One way to cut your hotel costs is to stay on the city's outskirts and there is a good selection in this category including the new Prince Philip at Kungens Kurva. It is close to a T-Bana station (19 minutes to the city centre). Off the E4 north of Stockholm is Mr Chips Hotel which almost adjoins the T-Bana (17 minutes to the centre). It gets its name not from the potato but from the silicon variety of chip. There are also two Scandics (at Hägersten and Kungens Kurva).

Destination Stockholm has some good packages which should be obtainable through UK travel agents. At the time of writing it was offering bed and breakfast plus a Stockholm Card for £16 to £31 per night, depending on hotel and location.

To do justice to Stockholm would take more than a few pages, but I hope I will have aroused your interest in this very fine city.

GOTHENBURG

GOTHENBURG *(Göteborg)* is Sweden's second largest city and its largest port and the principal point of entry for visitors with cars who have travelled by ferry from Britain. Situated on the Göta river, Gothenburg was founded in 1621 by King Gustavas Adolphus II who brought in Dutch experts to plan the city and they incorporated a series of canals and fortifications in their town plan.

The canals are still there and, together with the numerous parks, give the city an attractive quality and make it difficult to believe that it is a major industrial area.

Like Stockholm, there is a tourist card which is available for three periods of validity (prices at the time of writing, shown with the cost for children under 15 in brackets): 24 hours Skr65 (Skr35), 48 hours Skr95 (Skr60) and 72 hours Skr120 (Skr75). The Gothenburg Card can be obtained from the tourist offices at Kungsportsplatsen 2 and Nordstadstorget or Pressbyrån news-stands.

The card provides unlimited travel on local buses and trams and some rather restricted free car parking. It also lets you make a sightseeing coach tour, a trip on one of the Paddan canal boats and on the boat to the *Älvsborgs Fästning* (Elfsborg Fortress).

There is free entry to the huge Liseberg amusement park and to 11 museums. It also entitles you to a free trip to Denmark by Stena Line ferry and admission to a number of Gothenburg nightclubs.

Although it is a useful piece of plastic to have on your visit it does not compare in value with the excellent Stockholm Card.

The parking facilities provided by the Gothenburg Card are of course advantageous but having said that it must be added that Gothenburg is something of a nightmare in which to drive. Even Swedes cannot find their way around the city.

There is a leaflet available showing car parks and one-way streets and it is essential. The town map provided by the city tourist office is virtually useless to the motorist. I must add here that the Gothenburg Tourist Office really needs to get its act together because there are plenty of smaller towns with far superior facilities.

Taking the 50 minute city sightseeing bus tour would be a good way of getting some understanding of the city while an excursion on one of the Paddan boats is also well worthwhile. The latter takes you through the old canals, under 20 bridges and out into the harbour on a 55-minute round trip.

Apart from bus routes the basic public transport consists of nine tram routes, their focal point being Drottningtorget. These trams of course represent a further hazard for the unfortunate motorist visiting the city.

The city's main boulevard is the wide tree-lined *Kungsportsavenyn* – usually known simply as the Avenyn. At one end is *Götaplatsen* with the Concert Hall and the Gothenburg Museum of Fine Arts, the Municipal Library and the Municipal Theatre. In front of these buildings is Carl Milles' famous statue of Poseidon.

The Avenyn includes a number of hotels and restaurants and

shops and it stretches down past the *Stora Teatern* which is in park-like surroundings, near the *Rosenlundskanalen*. Beyond is *Kungsportsplatsen* and *Östra Hamngatan*, another shopping area. This street crosses *Stora Hamnkanalen*, the Great Harbour Canal.

Just to one side of Östra Hamngatan, by the canal, is Gustav Adolfs Torg – a cobbled flower-fringed square – where there is the Town Hall *(Rådhuset)*. The original building was completed in 1672 and rebuilt and extended in 1814–17. Not far away is the *Kronhuset*, the city's oldest secular building which was erected in 1643–55 as the arsenal. It was completely restored in 1957 and the building is now used for exhibitions and meetings and also includes a collection of city documents. Around Kronhuset is *Kronhusbodarna*, two rows of buildings dating back to 1759 which are now devoted to handicrafts and include little shops with a turn of the century atmosphere.

Fishing and shipping have both played a major part in the life and development of Gothenburg. There are daily fish auctions and there is a splendid retail fish market, the *Fiskhallen*, built in 1872–74, and often called the Fish Church because of its resemblance to a church. If you fancy deep sea fishing you can take day trips, the cost being between Skr110 and Skr150. The Maritime Museum *(Sjöfartsmuseet)* shows how the fishing and shipbuilding industries developed and it also incorporates an aquarium. There is an open air ship museum at Lilla Bommen which includes lightships, barges and also examples of Viking ships.

The city, as has already been mentioned, is well endowed with parks. The *Trädgårdsföreningens* Park is particularly nice; it was opened in 1842 when it was described as 'an oasis in the middle of the city'. It has a big hothouse – the *Palmhuset* – which was added in 1878. There is music and entertainment in the park in summer. The biggest park is *Slottskogen* which covers an area of 342 acres. It has beautiful walks and includes a children's zoo, two restaurants and a café. The Natural History Museum is also in this park.

The *Botaniska Trädgården* is another major park with 22 miles of roads and paths and has over 3,000 species of plants.

There are several locations from which good views of the city and the estuary can be obtained. Across the river from the city is Keillers Park, at Ramberget, which was donated to Gothenburg by a wealthy Scottish engineer, James Keiller. From the summit, 282 ft above sea level, you have a splendid view of the harbour. At Skansentorget is *Skansan Kronan*, a tower-like fort built in 1697 from whose ramparts there is a panoramic view of the city and the harbour entrance. The tower also includes a military museum with weapons and uniforms from the 17th century onwards. Another spectacular view can be obtained from the promontory where there is the *Masthuggskyrkan* (church) at Storebackegatan.

Ostindiska Huset, the former office building and warehouse of the Swedish East India Co., now houses the Archæological, Ethnographic and History Museums. Other museums include the

Röhsska Museum of Arts and Crafts, the Industrial Museum, the Museum of Medical History and Museum of Theatrical History.

As a complete contrast to museums take a boat trip to the *Nya Älvsborgs Fästning*, the New Älvsborg Fortress, which is a 16th century fortress strategically sited at the entrance to the harbour. It is a well-preserved and imposing structure and the boats leave from the Stenpiren. You can also go up the river to Vänersborg on the 'White Queen' and there are evening cruises to the archipelago on the old steamer 'Bohuslän', as well as day trips to Marstrand and Käringön.

The cathedral *(Domkyrkan)* is the third to be built in the city's history; the present building was completed in 1825 and is on the foundations of the previous two. The Örgryte Gamla Kyrka is a 13th century church which was extended in the 18th and 19th centuries and it has an impressive painted ceiling from 1741.

Gothenburg has a very good range of shops of all kinds from small boutiques to the large NK and Åhlens department stores. Nordstan is a major indoor shopping precinct near the railway station while behind Kungsportsplatsen is *Saluhallen*, a rather splendid food hall. For antiques and collectables there is *Antikhallarna* which has 25 to 30 shops under its roof and they cover everything from stamps to brassware.

The city is well-endowed with restaurants and cafés with those specialising in fish and seafood being well to the fore. There are also foreign restaurants which range from a French bistro to English-style pubs. There are several night spots which feature discos or live music and for an enjoyable evening you can't do better than *Liseberg*. This amusement park enjoys a spacious setting with trees, walks and floral displays. It has rides of all kinds from the old traditional type to the more recent awe-inspiring examples, sideshows, dancing, live entertainment, restaurants and cafés.

As the city plays host to many visitors attending major exhibitions and sporting events each year, it is well endowed with hotels. Among the bigger ones are the 480-room Europa (Sara group) which adjoins Nordstan shopping precinct; Gothia (also belonging to the Sara group and with 300 rooms); Park Avenue (SAS, 320 rooms and the most expensive); Opalen (Reso group with 237 rooms); and Rubinen (also Reso group with 189 rooms). Further out are the Scandinavia (Sara, 323 rooms); the Hotel Riverton (new, 207 rooms); Ramada (121 rooms); Panorama (360 rooms); and two Scandics (Backadal, 180 rooms and Mölndal, 218 rooms).

A very central and comfortable hotel which I can recommend is the Windsor which is on the 'Avenyn' and has 83 air-conditioned bedrooms, a good restaurant and bar. It also has the immense advantage of having its own underground car park.

The Gothenburg Package is a useful arrangement which includes bed and breakfast at a choice of hotels plus a Gothenburg Card. Prices at the time of writing ranged from Skr195 to Skr285. Details from the Tourist Bureau in the Kungsportsplatsen.

GOTLAND AND ÖLAND

GOTLAND IS THE largest island in the Baltic being about 75 miles in length and 35 miles at its widest point; it is roughly 50 miles from the Swedish mainland. Generally flat, the highest point is only 275 ft above sea level. There are frequent connections from the mainland by large ferries (see chapter on 'Ferries' for details).

The island is largely self-sufficient but tourism is important and there is a relatively short, hectic summer season. When I visited the island at the end of September it was very quiet and the excellent roads were virtually deserted. The scenery is a mix of shingle and sandy beaches; cliffs and meadows stretching down to the water; a somewhat barren landscape in the centre; and moorland and forest. The island has a comparatively mild climate throughout the year. Gotland is rich in wild flowers, especially orchids (36 varieties are to be seen) and attracts interesting species of birds. There are the semi-wild ponies called 'russ', but the predominating livestock are sheep.

The principal town, *Visby*, is probably the best reason for visiting Gotland. It was an important trading centre and a Hanseatic city, being at the peak of its importance in the 13th and 14th centuries. There is still two miles of the medieval city wall virtually intact and this is interspersed with 44 towers and numerous gates. Within the walled town there are the stepped gabled houses and a network of little streets which provide a unique atmosphere.

The original Hanseatic harbour – Almedalen – is now a park while the St. Maria Cathedral is the only medieval church in Visby that is still in use. There is an important Historical Museum *(Fornsalen)* which has an extensive collection of objects from the island's past. This 'town of roses' is well worth a visit although its many little one way streets make it a problem for driving. Congestion must be much worse in summer when Visby is full of visitors.

South of Visby at Tofta there is a good sandy beach and a little further south at Kronholmen is the island's only golf course. At the extreme southern tip at Hoburgen are the intriguing limestone stacks on the coast. If you then go north through the centre of the island you come to *Hemse*, the second largest town which is quite small. You then cross a comparatively barren area before coming to Roma and Romakloster, a 12th century ruined monastery.

North of Visby is *Lummelundagrottorna*, impressive limestone caves which are the island's most popular attraction. The northern end of the island is quite picturesque with an open air museum at Bunge. At Fårösund there is a ferry across to the adjoining island of Fårö. Unfortunately this northern area and the island are part of the Swedish defence zone. You need permission to visit Fårö, so see the tourist office in Visby before heading in that direction.

On the east coast the small town of Slite is dominated by the huge cement works which manages to spread a grey pallor over everything. Further south on the eastern side of the island there is a pleasant area which is largely overlooked by tourists. *Ljugarn* is an attractive little place with its seaside villas. The Ljugarn Pensionat is a suitable place to stay and the food, on my visit, was excellent.

The landscape is dotted with over 90 medieval churches and there are many relics from the past. While much of the scenery could not really be called 'pretty', it does have its own distinctive characteristics.

During the short summer season there is obviously plenty going on with entertainment and activities such as water skiing, riding and cycling but otherwise it is quiet. There are not a great many hotels compared with, for example, the Danish Baltic island of Bornholm. In Visby I stayed at the comfortable Bryggaregården which has 35 bedrooms but no restaurant. Nearby is Lindgården, which offers good food. Also in Visby is the Visby Hotel (92 rooms) and Donnersplats Hotel (20 rooms) both of which looked rather dull. There is plenty of self-catering accommodation, including holiday villages, and the island is also well served with camping sites and youth hostels.

Long and thin, *Öland* is Sweden's second largest island: 87 miles from north to south and 10 miles at its widest point. It is linked to the Swedish mainland by northern Europe's longest bridge. The biggest town is *Borgholm*, on the west coast, and nearby is *Solliden*, the Swedish Royal Family's summer residence (grounds open to the public) and the impressive castle ruins.

In the northern part of the island is the principal forested area and also the best beach around Böda bay. *Byxelkrok*, in the north-west is a fishing village and there is a nice stretch of coast to the south.

In the south is the Stora Alvaret, the distinctive treeless plain, 25 miles in length. Beyond it is *Eketorps Borg*, an ancient fortress from the 5th century which has now been reconstructed and is a fascinating centre. There are many things from the island's past: burial mounds and rune stones for example. Öland's most distinctive landmarks are the 400 windmills which are to be found all over the island (there were once 2,000 of them).

Also noticeable are the numerous medieval churches, many with defensive towers. The finest example is Gärdslösa church with its 12th century frescoes and 17th and 18th century decorations.

Other places of interest: Egby Kyrka (smallest church on the island); Störlinge Kvarnar – a row of seven windmills; Himmelsberga Hembygdsmuseum, two typical Öland farmhouses which now form a museum; Gråborg (the remains of an ancient fortress); Karlevistenen (the island's oldest rune stone from the 10th century); and Karl X Gustaf's wall – a stone wall built across the island in 1650.

The flora of Öland is remarkable and the island is, in particular, an orchid paradise with no less than 30 varieties to be found there. At Ottenby, in the extreme south, is the bird station which is of considerable interest to ornithologists.

HELPFUL GENERAL INFORMATION

Alphabet Instead of the usual 26 letters you will find the Swedish alphabet has 29. After A to Z comes Å, Ä and Ö. It is useful to remember this if you are referring to any kind of index or the telephone directory. The index in this guide is Swedish style.

Banks Normal opening hours are 9.30a.m. – 3.00p.m. Monday to Friday. Certain banks in Stockholm stay open until 5.30p.m. or 6.00p.m. All banks are closed on Saturdays.

British Embassy Skarpögatan 6–8, S–115 27 Stockholm. Telephone: (08) 67 01 40.

Chemist Called an Apotek. You can buy medicines for minor ailments without prescription but all other medications are on prescription. Normal opening hours are 9.00a.m. – 6.00p.m. Monday to Friday and 9.00a.m. – 12.00noon on Saturday. In towns the chemists work on a rota system and at least one will be open later and at weekends. Chemists do not sell toiletries or cosmetics.

Climate Because of the Gulf Stream Sweden has a temperate climate. It is broadly similar to the British climate but is frequently warmer and drier in summer – and colder in winter.

Currency The unit of currency is the Krona (plural Kronor). There are 100 öre in a Krona. Coins in circulation are 10 and 50 öre and 1Kr and 5Kr. Bank notes in circulation are: 10Kr, 50Kr, 100Kr, 500Kr, 1,000Kr and 10,000Kr. The abbreviation is usually shown as 'Kr' or 'Skr' (to differentiate between Swedish, Danish and Norwegian currencies); in banking it is abbreviated to SEK.

Electric current Throughout Sweden it is 220vAC, 50 cycles. Standard continental two-pin plugs are used so you will need an adaptor.

Emergencies Dial 90 000 from any public telephone (no charge).

Health service Britain has a reciprocal agreement with Sweden covering medical treatment which means that British citizens are entitled to the same service as Swedes. If you have a visit from a doctor the basic charge is Skr100 of which you can recover Skr40. You can go to the casualty department *(Akutmottagning)* or outpatients department *(Öppenvårdcentral)* at the nearest hospital *(Sjukhus)*. The fee for a hospital visit is Skr40. Always take your passport with you. If you have to stay in hospital there is no charge. Medicine on prescription is obtainable from a chemist (Apotek) and the maximum cost is likely to be Skr50. Travel insurance is also recommended.

Passports UK visitors to Sweden need to have a standard British passport or a British visitor's passport. A visa is not required.

Post office Normal opening hours 9.00a.m. – 6.00p.m. on weekdays and 10.00a.m. – 1.00p.m. on Saturday (some branches may close on Saturday in summer). Current postal rates (Sweden to UK) are Skr2.20 (postcard) or Skr2.70 (letter). You can buy stamps at most bookstalls. Over 500 post offices displaying the PK Exchange symbol can exchange foreign currency and travellers' cheques.

Public holidays Good Friday, Easter Monday, Labour Day (1 May), Ascension Day, Whit Monday, Midsummer's Day, All Saints' Day, Christmas Day, Boxing Day, New Year's Day and Epiphany. Offices and shops may also close or have earlier closing hours on the eve of a public holiday.

Radio news in English Radio Sweden International broadcasts 30 minutes of news, comment and information in the Greater Stockholm area (on 89.65 MHz FM) daily at 1.00 p.m., 2.30 p.m., 4.00 p.m., 6.00 p.m., 8.30 p.m., 11.00 p.m., 1.00 a.m., and 4.30 a.m. English language broadcasts can also be heard on medium wave.

Telephone Lift receiver, insert Skr1, wait for the dialling tone and dial your number. When you hear a signal during the call, it is time to insert more money. There are two types of public telephone in use, one which accepts Skr1 coins and the other taking 50 öre, Skr1 and Skr5 coins. For international calls dial 009 followed by the country code (44 for the UK) then wait for the second dialling tone before dialling the STD code and finally the subscriber's number. (Note: omit the first zero of the STD code – i.e. dial '1' for London, not '01'). Plenty of public telephones but not at post offices. There are also special offices, marked Tele or Telebutik.

Tipping Service charges are included on hotel and restaurant bills and you only tip if some special service has been rendered. You don't tip in washrooms or cloakrooms (where normally there is a fixed charge of Skr3 to Skr6) or cinema or theatre ushers. Taxi drivers expect 10 – 15% and at hairdressers it is optional.

Useful addresses

Swedish National Tourist Office, 3 Cork Street, London W1X 1HA. Telephone: 01-437 5816.

Swedish Tourist Board, Sverigehuset, Kungsträdgården, S–103 92 Stockholm. Telephone: (08) 789 20 00.

DFDS Seaways/Longship Holidays:

Scandinavia House, Parkeston Quay, Harwich, Essex CO12 4QG. Telephone: (0255) 554681.

Tyne Commission Quay, North Shields, Tyne and Wear NE29 6EE. Telephone: (091) 2575655.

DFDS Travel Centre, 199 Regent Street, London W1R 7WA. Telephone: 01-434 1523.

VAT Called 'Moms' in Sweden. The current rate is 19%. Normally all prices are shown VAT inclusive. About 8,000 shops participate in the Sweden Tax Free Shopping Service (see chapter on *Shopping*).

What you can take in Coming from the UK you can take into Sweden (if you are 15 years of age or over) 200 cigarettes or 100 cigarillos or 50 cigars or 9 oz (250 g) of tobacco and 200 cigarette papers. Visitors aged 20 or over can take in 1 litre of spirits, 1 litre of wine (or 2 litres if you don't take in any spirits) and 2 litres of beer.

INDEX

INDEX